Trans Boomer:

A Memoir of my Journey From

Female

to

Male

By Lee Jay

Edited by Emily May Anderson

The events in this book are true; however, there are some occurrences and conversations that I have had to create from memory. While all the events in the book are true, names and identifying details have been changed to protect the privacy of those involved.

ISBN: 978-1-62249-268-8

Published by
The Educational Publisher Inc.
Biblio Publishing
BiblioPublishing.com

DEDICATION

This book is dedicated to all of my foremothers and forefathers who fought, many with their lives, to help obtain the rights that I have today. Thank you for all that you have done to help my generation.

And to all of those worldwide who have lost their battle with AIDS: you will never be forgotten and the memories will never fade.

And to all those who are questioning their assigned birth gender: always remember you are beautiful and worthy of love. Follow your heart to become the person you wish to be. Always remember that you are never alone. Should you need to talk with someone, please call the Transgender Crisis Line: 877.656.8860.

PROLOGUE

An unexceptional day: I awake and begin my morning routine, while planning errands en route to a midday appointment. As I drive through a bustling intersection, a car speeds out of control from the opposite direction and strikes me head-on. I am squeezed unconscious, in the shattered ruins. Emergency Medical Services arrive on the scene, deftly extract me from the wreck, and wheel me into an ambulance. My condition is serious—head and face injuries, internal bleeding. Seconds after the ambulance technician stabilizes my oxygen mask, my blood pressure drops and my heart stops. The necessary documents for end of life matters have been written and recorded for decades; I consider it a part of responsible citizenship. My living will, my last will and testament, medical and financial powers of attorney all are on record. If my heart does not respond to the electrical shock and this is the end, I have had a great life.

What I have failed to prepare the emergency medical services technicians, doctors, and nurses for is the fact that I am transgender. Yes, I look, act, speak, dress, and live my life as an average male; however, under my clothes I have a female body.

ONE

As each of us journeys through life, the contemporary events of our time influence our life. This seems especially true for the largest generation to come of age in American history: the baby boomers. We were the post-World War II generation, born between 1946 and 1965, when America was wielding new influence in a postwar world. As youths, we rebelled against the Establishment, fought against race and gender inequality, protested the war in Vietnam, and supported sexual freedom within the context of economic prosperity. Our fathers were generally able to make more money and live better than their fathers, supported by stay-at-home wives.

In many ways, I was a quintessential baby boomer. I arrived late in 1957. President Dwight D. Eisenhower had been sworn in for a second term in January. During that year he asked Congress to authorize the use of U.S. armed forces against Communist aggression in Vietnam. The Soviet Union launched Sputnik, the world's first man-made satellite, into orbit around the earth. This began the "space race" and launched a frantic determination to improve public education. On the home front, Arkansas governor Orval Faubus, a staunch opponent of racial integration, defied a court decision when he ordered state militia troops to Little Rock, Arkansas to stop African-American students from entering a white school. The "separate but equal" court decision would prove to be the beginning of the movement for African-American civil rights.

At my birth, my mother was twenty-seven years old, and my father was thirty. My family would be completed with the birth of another baby girl four years later.

When I was almost four, my mother brought my baby sister home from the hospital with what seemed like endless scratches all over her tiny body. Perhaps they were signs of forceps used during her birth, or perhaps scratches from tiny nails before mittens had been secured over her roaming hands. I never asked about it, and my mother never discussed it, making me think it was more alarming for me than for adults. I wondered why my mother could not have picked out a child without any scratches. No one had told me that babies grew in their mother's wombs, and I thought that there were baby markets where mothers went and selected their offspring. I had never given any thought as to how the babies arrived at the baby market. Sexuality was a mystery to me, but I never gave it much thought at that age.

Even at age five, however, I had a nagging thought in my head that something was different inside of me. I did not understand what it was or why it was there, but I knew that I was different. I had no words to describe it. As I watched my younger sister start to grow and form her own personality, I began to see just how different I was. She was at home in her female body which made me aware of how uncomfortable I was in my mine. My body didn't match my thoughts of being a male. Perhaps, had my life been different, with liberal and emotionally available parents, I might have voiced my confusion. However, this wasn't possible with my parents and their rigid gender expectations. They wanted a feminine female who followed society's demands for the stifling and limiting gender roles that were present during the early sixties. Women were to be in the home raising children and supporting their husband's careers. This was to be my fate as well in my parent's eyes, and I was appalled that this was the only option provided to me. Knowing that, I was secretive about the fact that I desired something different. My mother provided a constant review of how females were to be soft and dainty, almost barely present. Being constantly reminded to take small "girl" steps made me self-conscious, when my gait seemed naturally male and I lumbered along in a dress that wasn't meant for me. Yet, I had no role models, no descriptive vocabulary, and nowhere to turn to find any support in my confusion.

My sister and I would take opposite paths in our lives; however, I was always grateful that I had a sibling. She would stay in our hometown, marry and raise children, while I would leave and come of age within the gay world in a large city. Her story is hers alone to tell; however, I was proud to be the firstborn and took that role seriously throughout my entire life.

Both of my parents brought their own agendas into my life, as all parents do. My mother was born in 1930 into rural poverty, to parents who were attempting to scratch out an existence during the Great Depression. They owned ten acres in the Great Lakes region, complete with a few cows, pigs, and chickens. I listened to my mother talk of how she had to milk the cows every day, and how chickens would run around even after their heads had been cut off. She knew how to call the pigs and fetch fresh eggs. Most of all, she talked of how difficult it was to tend to the livestock and gardens, with the never-ending, demanding physical labor that required. Every member of the family had chores to complete as a team to ensure that things ran as smoothly as possible.

During the Great Depression, it was not uncommon for children to run away and ride the rail cars, or for men who were unable to support their families to desert them. Also, large families were forced to farm out their children to relatives who had more resources. This was the case in my mother's family, which had four children, born one to two years apart. My mother was second oldest. She and her older sister were sent to live with an aunt in a large city, when they were six and seven years old. My mother was homesick for her mother, and returned to the farm after a year. My aunt stayed in the city, where she had a much easier life.

As the oldest daughter now, my mother took care of eventually five younger siblings while her parents were tending the crops. They had no indoor plumbing or electricity; a wood-burning, pot-bellied stove provided heat for the rundown farm house on ten acres of land. Life was beyond difficult.

Years later, when I was a young child, my mother would drive my sister and me out into the country twenty miles away, to the farmhouse to see my grandmother. I loved visiting. I thought the cars in the front yard, some on blocks, and some just rusting, were beautiful. I would climb into them and imagine that I was a teenage boy on a race track. Weeds and snakes surrounded the house, which leaned noticeably to one side. A pump in the front yard produced water which fascinated me. The walls were covered with road maps, given away free at the gas stations and used in place of wallpaper or paint. The only toilet was an old outhouse around the back of the house, among outbuildings in various stages of decay.

Across the street was a seedy truck stop owned by a large country woman with long, white hair, who was both manager and waitress. Her sons would urinate in their front yard; I knew this was the stance that males used to urinate because I had accidently seen my father in the same position while I was running past the open bathroom door on my way down the stairs. I would stare in disbelief at their openness. This was the rural poverty that my mother had escaped by getting married the first chance she got. It was her only way out at the time.

My mother self-identified as a "depression baby," which would affect her all her life. I am grateful for many of the lessons that she taught me as a child. For example, she never threw anything away; everything was repaired and recycled. She clipped coupons, saved Green Stamps, and never paid full retail price. She would dress in sweaters rather than turning up the heat. She saved water and reused it whenever possible; we hung clothes outside on the clothesline in three seasons and in the basement during the winter. There was no air conditioning, no garbage disposal, not even trash bags. We put food waste in paper grocery bags and took it daily to the garbage cans. I have always lived that way, and I was later surprised to discover that many Americans did not.

In 1955 my mother married my father, whom she met while living in a rooming house that his parents owned. On the other hand, my father was born in a working-class neighborhood of a large city. His father was deaf by the age of twelve, but never learned American Sign Language. He taught himself to lip read, and worked in a factory. My father, like my mother, wanted out of the life that he had been born into. Factories and the big city were not for him. He wanted a better life in a small town, away from the pollution, grime, and crowded neighborhoods. He moved to a small town after graduating from high school, and worked as a valet in a successful hotel located on a bustling and profitable old-time Main Street as his first job.

My father's mother had died before I was born. She was diabetic, and had died from complications of the disease. I never knew what year she died; it was never discussed. The rest of his family, which included his older brother and sister, and his father, would eventually move to the Southwest before I was born. In the few times that I saw my grandfather before his death, he was frail and asthmatic, with two hearing aids, and legs covered with ulcers. He wore glasses, and supported himself with a cane. I never knew him well or had much conversation with him.

My father's next job was at Sears, Roebuck & Company. He was a salesman in the furniture and floor covering department, paid on commission and given a gasoline allowance. My father was a raging alcoholic, but a born salesman. I started to notice his drinking at age seven; a constant beer in his hand whenever he was home, with behavior changes occurring as the disease progressed. When he was drinking his rage and disgust would surface and he was not to be trusted. He would begin his verbal abuse about how hard he worked and how little we cared, or how we had wasted his money somehow. He was a functional alcoholic: he knew he had to keep his job to pay for his alcohol and always managed to stay employed. There had been very little public discussion of alcoholism, or the effects it had on the drinker and his or her family and employment, despite the fact that Alcoholics Anonymous had been formed in 1935.

Phil Donahue began broadcasting his talk show in 1967, when I was ten. Donahue was the first to discuss topics that had been taboo in American society. He would foster discussions that were educational, full of exploration and learning. But at this time I knew nothing of alcoholism, and the denial and lying that were often involved, let alone the financial disasters and extramarital affairs that characterized my father's life. I always knew that he drank too much, because he and my mother argued the point again and again. He was able to control his addiction when I was young; however, by the time I was a teenager he was losing the battle. He maintained a double life, but more people in our small town knew that he was an alcoholic and when drunk in public exhibited deplorable behavior. My father, during work hours, associated with men just like him: alcoholics who also had mistresses and felt that they deserved them. After all, they were supporting a wife and children and felt it was a perk of the job. My father was in the company of men who shared his philosophy on married life; male privilege allowed men to share time with their family and their mistress.

I would receive reports from my friends at school who overheard their parents discussing my father's activities in his other life. Everyone in our neighborhood all went to the same school together so the community was very small and very few activities were that private. One night he would be thrown out of a bar because he would not stop verbally abusing the female staff, the next week he would be buying his mistresses' children all new clothes, the next week scheduling a decoy "sales meeting" in a hotel near the city with another mistress in tow. He would spend money faster than he could earn it: the alcohol, supporting his many mistresses and their families, the hotel rooms for meetings that were needed to provide false secrecy. By some miracle he was never charged with driving under the influence of alcohol, at least not that I was aware of.

He considered himself a modern man and insisted on the newest toys on the market, furniture, clothes, and appliances. My mother was just the opposite, never replacing an item until it was worn beyond repair. These extreme differences in money spending allowed for endless arguments.

My father made an excellent salary, without a college degree and only on-the-job training. He came of age during booming economic times long before investor "bubbles," downsizing, and outsourcing. He never had to worry about age discrimination, or his company going bankrupt. He was the sole breadwinner and like many alcoholics, demanded perfection from others, yet lived a double life. I learned at a very young age never to trust him when the alcohol took over. However, he was an excellent provider. I was enrolled in the best public school that my small town offered. Make no mistake; I am grateful for all that he provided. However, I do hold him accountable for the abuse that he gave to my family and chose not to tolerate his behavior once I became an adult. He never accepted any accountability, always believing he was right and I only a child, no matter what my age.

As I have mentioned, my parents married in 1955. Both parents had seen no combat duty or indeed, any direct involvement in World War II or the Korean War. Like most newlyweds of their time, they purchased a home in 1955. The cost was ten thousand dollars. I am sure they were excited and hopeful at that time. The house was large, containing a full basement, two large bedrooms, an eat-in kitchen, living room, and dining room, situated on a large lot. I loved my neighborhood. There were children in almost every house. Mine was one of the smallest families on the street; many of my neighbors had three to seven children. I formed bonds with some of my neighbors that would last a lifetime. As an adult, I look back with the fondest of memories on those who grew up with me, walked to school with me, and graduated with me. We were within walking distance of a farmer's market, gas stations, convenience stores, and my beloved junior high school. As an adult, I bought my own home in the exact same sort of neighborhood: within walking distance of everything I would need, and one block away from a school.

TWO

One of the most influential elements of my childhood was that I was born into the Jehovah's Witnesses religion.

The inception of Jehovah's Witnesses was in 1874, when Charles Taze Russell founded the organization that was first coined the International Bible Student's Association. Upon Russell's death in 1916, Joseph Rutherford assumed the presidency, concentrating on increasing membership. He died in 1942, and was quickly and quietly replaced by Nathan Knorr, under whose leadership I spent my early life living as a Witness and a member of the now-incorporated Watchtower Bible and Tract Society. I was the third generation of Jehovah's Witness on both my parent's lineage. My father would lead a double life for years; male privilege and patriarchy were staples of the religion so it was easy for him.

Jehovah's Witnesses, like many other minority sects, are foremost separatist and isolationist. Their lives are very different from their neighbor's lives; there are scriptural doctrines passed down from the governing authority that must be followed without question. Any violation of these doctrines, based on scriptural content, results in the shunning of the violator. As in many sects that control their members' lives, the individual is relatively unimportant; the group is all important. Throughout my life I have always preferred to belong to a group. I feel most secure when connected to other humans.

People turn to religion for comfort, a tradition to follow, and answers to the questions of meaning that humanity seeks. That is a forte of Jehovah's Witnesses: all of the answers are in the scriptures. This method of learning produces black-and-white thinking, with no discussion of any kind. I was instructed in The Watchtower and Bible Tract Society's interpretation of the Bible. I was taught how to present that interpretation to others, including outreach work that involved knocking on doors in the community. This was done to spread the word of God to all who would listen. If I did not do this, their blood would be on my hands when the Battle of Armageddon occurred. I was responsible for their lives and for introducing to them the true teachings of God.

Growing up as a Jehovah's Witness was an experience different from anything I have ever known. In fact, I would not expect anyone to fully understand my situation unless they, too, had been born into a religion with a similar outlook and approach to teaching. My early life provided me with lessons that I still carry with me: helping others, treating others like you would prefer to be treated, and fighting injustices. The Watchtower Bible and Tract Society was a very controlled social world that revolved around my family and congregation. Parents were responsible for rearing their children in the discipline of Jehovah, their God. The status that the parents enjoyed in the world of the congregation depended on how well their children matured and whether they remained active within the religion. If children left the religion, the parents experienced shame and embarrassment.

From birth, the children attended all functions and events in the congregation; when children were old enough to comprehend, they were taught the guiding principles of Armageddon. Armageddon was a war between God and Satan, which would bring worldwide destruction, death, and persecution to all of Jehovah's Witnesses. The timeline for this war was always imminent, but with no actual date defined. Therefore, children were taught to be obedient, and parents studied the Bible with their children for hours to teach the doctrines. By age five, children accompanied their parents to "field service work," which involved knocking on homeowners doors in a designated neighborhood to teach the "Word of God."

The Watchtower Bible and Tract Society judged success by how much literature a member of the family placed in the hands of the public, and ultimately, how many who showed an interest in the literature would make a commitment to begin Bible studies. Children and adults kept track of hours spent proselytizing to others, and this information was then sent to the headquarters of the organization, located in Brooklyn, New York. The more hours spent at worship and the more publications "placed" (never sold) with nonbelievers, the more credit upon the parents. After all, the Bible orders parents to bring their children up in the discipline of Jehovah. It was more than a responsibility; the children's actual blood was on the parents' hands if they failed. To lose a child to "the world" out of Jehovah's flock was to scar their record as parents and Christians.

Witnesses took great care, therefore, to isolate children from the outside world. Public education was a requirement for some parents; many chose to home school their children. Parents who used public schools denigrated them by emphasizing that only The Watchtower Bible and Tract Society ("The Society") taught "the truth." The world was not going to go on, because God would step in and the battle of Armageddon would begin. In fact, parents told their children they would not graduate, because Armageddon would arrive far sooner than the end of a public school education. Children who rebelled against the doctrines received swift and harsh punishment. (The biblical concept of "spare the rod and spoil the child" was taken literally.) Children entering high school were channeled into vocational education, toward a job with minimal responsibilities, because that would then allow full-time service and proselytizing. A college education was forbidden, as was any sort of career. A job was secondary to serving Jehovah.

Being an active Jehovah's Witness was a full-time job for good reason: there was no time to think, question, or stray from doctrine. Only men were allowed to speak to the congregation. Both patriarchy and scriptural doctrine supported this rule. Men were heads of families, with women and children in a subservient position. There was a one-hour Bible study on Tuesday nights, a two-hour meeting on Thursday nights, and a two-hour meeting on Sunday mornings. In addition, members were expected to engage in field service for a minimum of two hours on Sundays, Wednesdays, and Saturdays. Family Bible study within the home took a minimum of two to three hours per week. The weekly schedule included personal family Bible study on Monday night for at least an hour. Tuesday night meant a trip to a private home for an hour of Bible study.

For seven years the Tuesday night Bible study was conducted in my parent's home. My mother required that the house be spotless, and my sister and I both assisted with the chores. I was always grateful for the cleaning and organizational skills that my mother taught me. I never considered cleaning to be a chore; I enjoyed a clean environment. The yard would be immaculate as well; my summer holidays were spent working in the yard. While the rest of the world was celebrating Memorial Day, Independence Day and Labor Day, I would be weeding the gardens. There was always something to keep us busy. I assisted in setting up folding chairs in the living room to accommodate the fifteen members who would begin to arrive around 7:45 in the evening with the meeting beginning at 8:00 P.M.

Despite the lack of air conditioning, the customary dress code specified suits and ties for men, with women in dresses and skirts. The meeting began with a prayer by a man, followed by reading a textbook dictated by the Society. The topic could be a discussion of the book of Revelation as the Society interpreted the content. There would be round robin reading by males and females of one paragraph in the textbook, followed by questions on the material just read. The Society orchestrated all of the content, questions, and Bible scriptures. When the elder asked questions, everyone was encouraged to raise his or her hand and answer. For many years my father was in charge of the Tuesday night Bible study. Of course, because of this my sister and I were to set the example and always be prepared to raise our hands to answer some of the questions. After the hour-long meeting, prayer would conclude the event, with socializing to follow.

There were times when my father would need to discuss a private topic with another elder attending the meeting. When this happened, the females were herded into another room. All topics the elders discussed were secret, even from their wives. When this happened, I was permitted to accompany the women into the other rooms and listen to their conversations. Many times, conversations revolved around recipes or how to save money at the grocery. I was not permitted to engage in the conversation, but I was proud to be there. This signaled a rite of passage for me. I learned a lot by just listening to the women discussing household tips.

Wednesday morning required a minimum of two hours in field service, or knocking on doors in the community to announce Jehovah's Kingdom. On Thursday, we went to the Kingdom Hall for two hours. Friday could be a day off, perhaps, or more personal family Bible study. Saturday mornings, members again spent a minimum of two hours in field service, knocking on doors again. Sunday was an all day affair, with two hours of meetings at the Kingdom Hall and at least two hours of field service work. What was taught during the hours and hours of lecturing? Why, how to live a Christian life, of course!

The public sermon on Sundays would include a topic structured to be of general interest to the mainstream public, in hopes that some of the people "of the world" whom the Witnesses had spoken to during the weekly field service work would visit. In addition, Sunday brought question-and-answer study of *The Watchtower*, the companion magazine to *Awake!*, both of which were given to nonmembers who showed interest. The Thursday night program was called The

Theocratic Ministry School, in which everyone in the congregation was given a topic to research and present. The men spoke directly to the congregation, whereas women sat on the stage facing each other. Topics included biblical history or scriptural doctrine.

For example, I might be assigned the topic: "Why Jehovah's Witnesses refuse blood transfusions." I and another female congregant would meet in a hypothetical hospital waiting room. I would act the role of a Witness explaining to someone "of the world" why, based on scriptural content, I had just told a doctor that my mother was not to be given a blood transfusion under any circumstances. These assignments were posted on a bulletin board located at the back of the Kingdom Hall. Members would have a month to six weeks to prepare. The discussion took place at a small table, on a small stage, with microphones, in front of the congregation. There would be a five-minute time limit. Afterward, I would be graded on particular aspects of public speaking, such as gesturing, volume, and vocabulary. The Society controlled everything in the religion: what doctrines would be discussed, what scriptures would accompany every sermon, and even the songs that had to be sung from their songbook. There was no deviating from what was sent down from the Watchtower and Bible Tract Society.

I started public speaking at about age nine or ten, and to this day it comes very easily to me. The Witnesses provided a "Toastmaster" group of sorts, and I excelled in it and acquired a lifetime skill. It also taught me another advantage, the ability to sell and overcome rejection. During those endless meetings at the Kingdom Hall, overcoming rejections in field service work was discussed repeatedly. They provided a scripture or a scripted response to every objection a householder could give. I was taught never to expose my true emotions, with the ultimate goal of placing *The Watchtower* and *Awake!* into my host's hands. Later, Witnesses would make a follow-up visit with the goal of getting the person to attend Bible study and eventually convert to the religion.

Some of the Witnesses' beliefs affected me more deeply than others. Jehovah's Witnesses do not celebrate any holidays or birthdays. They are conscientious objectors, refusing to participate in any war or nationalistic endeavors. This includes saluting a flag or singing the national anthem. They are anti-abortion, anti-homosexuality, and anti-smoking. They do not believe in blood transfusions or organ donations. The religion supports patriarchy, with the husband to be obeyed as God is obeyed. In addition, any member who knows that another member is sinning or participating in any violations is under scriptural orders to report him or her to a committee of elders.

There was not only a hint of fascism; there was a Gestapo as well. If another congregant saw me walking anywhere in my small town, he or she reported it to my parents. If fellow congregants suspected someone was violating the rules, they reported it. Paranoia prevailed at every turn, as a way to keep the congregation "clean from wrongdoers." In other words, this free, homemade policing service helped people in authority know what was happening with members. Of course, there was a scriptural doctrine to justify this action. In addition, the person doing the reporting had a sense of pride in knowing they were doing their part to keep the organization clean from anyone who failed to follow all the rules. Living in a small town where everyone knew everyone else ensured that my life was constantly monitored and discussed with my mother, who provided the punishment for anything not allowed in God's organization.

There are some things about my upbringing for which I am grateful. First, I was raised in an unprejudiced household. There were only "the sheep and the goats," Jehovah's people and "the world." No groups of people were singled out for hatred. Also, I was raised in an international milieu. My parent's home resembled an international hotel, with missionaries from every corner of the globe seeking lodging or meals. I also traveled most of the North American continent attending "assemblies." My mother enjoyed American history, and arranged tours of historical sites during these trips. I loved major cities that were alive with diversity. The two cities that meant the most to me as a child were New York City and San Francisco.

Assemblies were week-long conventions for Jehovah's Witnesses, Monday through Sunday, usually housed in baseball stadiums redecorated by volunteers for the occasion. They were always on the weekends during the school year but not in the summer. My first one was in 1958, barely a year old, when a quarter of a million Witnesses from around the globe packed both Yankee Stadium and the adjacent Polo Grounds. I experienced assemblies as brutal; sermons would run from 9 am to 9 pm, with only two one-hour breaks for lunch and dinner. The volunteer labor involved to produce these events was enormous. Men took their annual vacations to work and attend the assemblies; entire families like my own volunteered. I was ten when I mopped the floor after an assembly-line baptism at a high school pool. I worked in food service and directing crowds. Children as well as adults were expected to work, with volunteerism a part of the event. As a group, Jehovah's Witnesses were extremely poor; thus, working hard was a badge of honor as well as an expectation. I learned to follow orders without question.

My religion, then, was more than a religion–it was a way of life that dictated everything I did. It would haunt me when I tried to leave it behind. I have spent a lifetime trying to catch up on what I had missed in a world so isolated from the general population. I struggled to blend in at my job or in social situations, never quite sure if I was interacting the way the rest of the world seemed to know how to do. I would surreptitiously study everything around me, looking for clues. In time, I could act my way through most social situations, by being personable, observant, and submissive. I tried to be low key and not stand out.

Another aspect of my life that would haunt me was my health. I was born into a gene pool with a multitude of health problems. Addictions prevailed on both sides of my family. Cancer and mental illness were rampant on my mother's side. My maternal grandfather had multiple sclerosis, and died of a stroke. My maternal grandmother had died of uterine cancer in her early sixties. My paternal grandmother had diabetes and was dead long before I was born.

I had some congenital defects: I was born with no eustachian tubes in my ears, a double ureter on my right side, and poor eyesight. The worst problem of all was my weak immune system. I was plagued with ear infections, strep throat, and sinus infections all my life. From my public school years to my adult employment, health care would always be an expense. When I was a child, my father complained about how much my medical bills cost. I was in the hospital for the first time when I was five years old, getting my tonsils out in the hope of preventing more ear infections. (It didn't help.)

My public school education began in the fall of 1963. I almost missed attending kindergarten, because my classroom was going to be housed within a church basement. Because Jehovah's Witnesses were never to enter any other church for any reason, I almost was forbidden to attend. I remember my mother talking to the women in the congregation about the situation, bemoaning the fact that the overcrowding had occurred in my first year. Eventually, space opened within the school building by the beginning of the school year, and I was allowed to attend my full year of kindergarten in public school.

THREE

By 1960, a new chapter started with a new decade of American history. John F. Kennedy was elected by a narrow margin over Richard Nixon. He was the youngest president to date. His wife, Jackie, spoke fluent Spanish and French. She was a former debutante from Boston, and the Kennedy family was Catholic. America was quite enamored with the Kennedys. Jackie soon set the fashion stage for women. Jackie and my mother were the same age; I was Caroline's age, and my younger sister was the same age as John Jr. My mother became a collector of all things Jackie Kennedy. She kept endless scrapbooks, folders of newspaper clippings, crude as they were with blotchy black-and-white photos, and a library of books as the years went on.

My mother would often dress me like Caroline Kennedy. After all, we were peers, and my mother, along with most of the nation, dressed like Jackie Kennedy. As children, we lived as though we were in the White House as well. Our wardrobe was always perfect, with our speech mature and adult-like. I learned at an early age how to shake hands with an elder and carry on an adult conversation.

We entertained people from all around the world who visited our home. There were missionaries from other parts of the world coming to visit members in the congregation or an elder who was visiting from another state. My mother hosted formal dinner parties based on the Jackie Kennedy guide to entertainment. There were many photo shoots in the country's various magazines detailing all things Kennedy. My mother read all of them and saved the articles as well. My father would provide gifts of watches or other male jewelry to the men, while the women would share food recipes with my mother.

The entire house was always obsessively cleaned in every room along with the garage and yard. We were ready to host at a moment's notice. I enjoyed this most when I was allowed to wear slacks rather than a dress when dinners were less formal. Although children were to be silent unless spoken to, I enjoyed the relaxed sense of community that was present during these times.

In our nation this was that shining moment when all things were Camelot. America was at the cusp of a new decade, embracing a new chapter. We were ready to tackle our problems together with unity and pride. In his inaugural address, Kennedy stated to the country, "And so, my fellow Americans, ask not what your country can do for you–ask what you can do for your country." That statement was quoted on the entrance of our police station and I would read it each time I passed, believing in the meaning of public service. Although my parents shared their resources to help others, voting was not permitted under Witness doctrine. Any sort of civic involvement was forbidden as well. These actions would violate scriptural doctrine, which quoted Jesus as saying that his followers were no part of this world. Thus, Jehovah's people would be no part of the world. My mother's admiration of the Kennedy family would stop at politics. However, I started kindergarten in the fall of 1963 knowing, in an elementary sort of way, that there was optimism and hope prevailing in the country.

Every baby boomer remembers where they were on that fateful day, November 22, 1963. We all remember the disbelief and shock of the news reports coming out of Dallas. There were tears and horror. We watched the film of Jackie Kennedy crawling across the trunk of the convertible limousine as Secret Service agents sought to protect her. Her husband slumped beside her, with blood everywhere. America lost its innocence that day. We had survived the Cuban missile crisis just a year earlier, never thinking that our young president, full of life and promise, would be gunned down before our eyes. Within two days, many of us would witness another murder when Jack Ruby gunned down Lee Harvey Oswald on live television.

My memory is cloudy on the assassination itself, but I remember that Sunday vividly. I was playing in the dining room of my childhood home, while my mother washed dishes in the kitchen. Suddenly my father screamed at the television in the living room. My mother rushed in from the kitchen, wiping her hands on a towel. My father was yelling that Lee Harvey Oswald had just been shot. I remember that moment as vividly as my first day of school, and thus began my fascination with the Kennedy assassination. The nation watched the funeral as John Jr. saluted his father's coffin as it passed. We wiped tears from our eyes and watched the courage, grace, and dignity that Jackie displayed throughout the entire ordeal. The pain ran deep; after all, we had an intimate relationship with the Kennedy clan. I remember watching television with my mother as the funeral procession made its way through our nation's capital. My mother would follow Jackie Kennedy's life after the White House, as I would follow all of the Kennedys' lives.

On the first day of school, I would inform my teachers that I was not to salute the flag, sing the national anthem, or celebrate any birthdays or holidays within the school setting. They would handle the situation with grace and respect. I loved my teachers, and I loved school.

Before having children, my mother had worked full time at an office of a local business, but quit when she became pregnant. This is what women were expected to do during that era: embrace motherhood and domesticity. When I learned of this, I found myself wishing she had remained working at her career. I could see the isolation and dependence on the male paycheck that this created. Also, because of these actions there was an automatic imbalance of power. Women gave up so much in the fifties and sixties to have their children and stay at home to raise them. Historically, that was what was done at the time and I wished my mother could have stayed at her position part time just to keep her skills up in the marketplace. I also wished that my mother had wanted some sort of advanced education, a skill that would help her achieve financial independence when it would be needed. I had a strong passion for learning which my mother did encourage but on a limited basis. Priorities in learning started with the Bible, and if there was any time after that, historical reading was allowed.

I had only been separated from my mother once, when my younger sister was born. Since the fathers at that time were frequently wedded to their careers and not familiar with child care needs, I went to another family's house to stay. I had fun playing hide and seek with the other children, but still felt anxious. On my first day of school, I was terrified to leave my mother. My mother did not work outside the home, and I had always stayed at home with her without the company of peers. She would tell me that I would accompany her throughout the day through the house as she did her housework, went to the grocery, and completed her errands. She would constantly engage me in all that she was doing, but it was only she and I together. My first trip into the world without her by my side was difficult. I was fine once I got into my classroom because I was in an excellent school district and had above-average teachers. In all of my years of public education, I only once had a bad teacher. I was never molested, and I was paddled more than once.

From about age five, I had known on a subconscious level that I was different in many ways from the children around me. The other children seemed to be comfortable in their given gender roles while I was not, especially when it came to the clothes I had to wear. It never bothered me that I missed all the holiday and birthday parties. Jehovah's Witnesses didn't celebrate them based on scriptural doctrine. Since my family never celebrated holidays, they were a foreign concept to me. However, I was acutely aware that I felt and I'm sure looked awkward in my new dress. I was not able to walk gracefully and take small steps; I was taller than all of my classmates, thin, and always impulsive in my actions. I was frequently absent, sick at home with another ear infection, strep throat, or some sort of influenza. Therefore, I never gained the social experience that the early school years provide. School in the early years provides a student with many things in addition to social development. There is the academic content that is a prerequisite to all future skills needed to read, write and perform advanced math skills. There are also fine and gross motor skills that are developed in those early years through physical education and the art classes. Gross motor skills are learned in physical education with ball games and fine motor skills involve learning to properly use a pair of scissors. Students also learn organizational skills, sequencing skills and the ability to follow multiple-step directions. Attendance is crucial to master all of what is taught to children throughout their school career. Because I was sick and absent for a third of the school year, every year throughout my elementary school grades of kindergarten through sixth grade, I didn't learn all of the skills that I should have simply because I was not at school.

Although I would go from kindergarten through third grade before I had to deal with the schoolyard bullies, I always felt generalized fear and anxiety in every situation throughout the day. Because I missed so much school, I didn't have the stability that my classmates had. After all, they were there every day, had formed their circle of friends who would eat lunch together and play on the playground together. I, on the other hand, would start to bond with someone and then be gone for a week or two because I was home sick. Having never attended preschool or daycare, school was scary in the beginning. Also, I was anxious knowing that I felt male inside my mind but was trying to be female. I was worried my classmates would sense that I was different. I had trouble asking for help when I needed it.

Once, I was afraid to ask permission to use the bathroom before I left the classroom and of course did not make it home before I had an accident. I was walking home alone that day, and felt burning shame. My mother met me half way on my route walking home in a urine soaked dress and tights. My walk to school was almost a mile and my mother would meet me half way to help with the transition. She could not understand why I had not asked to use the restroom before I had left. I was unable to verbalize that it was the end of the school day, everyone was preparing for dismissal and it was hectic. I had been hesitant to ask because my teacher seemed to be so busy; after all, she was responsible for thirty-three young children. I did not want to interrupt her and I thought I had the situation under control. The thought had never occurred to me to interrupt my teacher with my needs because I thought it would have been disrespectful. Every child has accidents in the early years of school and I was more troubled by it than my mother.

At the end of each year, we were administered our standardized tests. I always missed questions because I was unable to wait long enough to listen to the directions. The following year, I continued to have trouble because I would not take time to read the directions. I was always in a hurry to complete a task without stopping to think. When my mother questioned me as to why I was unable to control my behavior, I always thought I was stupid because I could not do better at controlling my impulses. Of course, at five and six years old, I was unable to verbalize my thoughts. My mother would ask me why I couldn't attempt to complete things at a slower pace and I didn't know how to respond. However, I set myself to those high perfect standards and I have struggled throughout my life with lack of focus before diving head first into something.

I wanted everything to be perfect—as both of my parents were perfectionists themselves. If I could jump into something quickly enough I would have time to make it perfect, or so I thought. I was also unable to leave anything unfinished; thus, I would dive in just to be able to complete the task and mark it off of my list. This pattern was applied to everything in my life. Because I felt that I had so many deficits, this was my way of excelling. I had missed so much school and missed out on developing so many skills in all domains. In addition, I felt as though I was in the wrong body and was worried that everyone could witness my confusion at trying to be female. I wanted to be able to excel at something to save my self esteem. Furthermore, I wanted to be perfect so people would like me: I was an outcast on so many levels, and I longed for acceptance as part of the normal mainstreamed student body.

Being different was an open invitation for bullying and in adulthood, discrimination. I attended school during a time when discussions on differences were barely discussed. The focus was on academics and not on social development during the early sixties. Conformity was still important; this was before the rebellion of youth in the late sixties. Authority was still respected and not questioned: this applied at home and at school. Praise wasn't something that my parents knew anything about and no doubt their parents knew nothing of it as well. I was the one to try and examine my strengths and weaknesses. I was the one to begin to observe where I could excel and where I would struggle.

My teachers would provide praise and counsel when I needed it and this helped me tremendously.

FOUR

In our house, my parents were constantly arguing. To protect myself, I attempted to make everything perfect in order to stay out of the adult conflict. My mother always stressed that I was the first born and needed to be the mature one to set the example for my younger sister. My sister on the other hand was always joking about the situation, and the comic relief was always welcome. She and I both loved to focus on the way people talked: various speech patterns, accents, or favorite words. At night, in our respective twin beds, we would imitate the speech, complete with exaggeration where fitting, and find it entertaining. We continued this into our adult lives and it was how we bonded.

My mother struggled with depression that frequently found its way into anger and despair. There were times when I would dread coming home from school because when I opened the door, I did not know what mood was going to greet me. My mother was swift and hard in her discipline, because that was the pattern of child rearing she had seen throughout her childhood. There was no public discussion on parenting then like there would be in later years. Parents frequently modeled what they had experienced with their parents.

She had had a very hard-working childhood on a farm; we were now living in a comfortable suburb. With no cows to milk or gardens to tend to, my life was much too easy and free. Each generation looks back at their lives and feels that the current generation has it easier. After all, she had lived through the Great Depression and I was living in one of the most prosperous times in history. As an adult, I would find myself in that same situation, looking at the current generation with so many more opportunities. In addition, my mother had been the victim of schoolyard teasing because she dressed like a farmer, not a city girl. Because of those experiences, she dressed my sister and me in very stylish clothes purchased on sale at the department stores. A perfect appearance meant that the behavior was to be perfect as well, especially for Jehovah's Witnesses. We were an example to our God, and everything was a reflection upon Jehovah. I learned at a young age to be respectful, kind, and considerate, but the best dress in the store did not make me feel like a girl.

I knew from a young age never to say that to my mother—to say such a thing out loud would result in punishment. Scriptural doctrine declared homosexuality to be a sin in many religious sects, and Jehovah's Witnesses were no different. In my heart, I always knew I was different and all of those around me thought it sinful and disgusting. There were articles published in the literature created by The Watchtower Bible and Tract Society on this very issue. The scripture was always the same: "men who lie with men will not inherit God's kingdom." Everyone I had ever met in my life would have the same opinion: it was sinful and against God's and nature's laws. When someone who was in a family broke Jehovah's law, shunning would be enforced by both family members and the congregation, unless that person who broke God's law repented.

Instead of nightly prayers to ask God to change me, I instead chose to keep my thoughts to myself. I did wish that my voice would not be as deep because it added to the gender confusion along with my height. If I was supposed to be female, why was I given these obviously male traits? My mother no doubt wondered as well since my younger sister had none of these differences. Being a baby boomer and born during the fifties resulted in a different set of parents than we have today. Times were different; homosexuality was illegal and still a mental illness, with no mother wanting this life for their child. In the Watchtower Bible and Tract society, my entire world since birth, rules were strict, rules were always followed, and rules were never questioned. Breaking the rules meant shame upon my family, embarrassment, and a mark against my parents.

In my parent's home, television was censored. I was not permitted to watch any violent television shows. My father never hunted, so there were no firearms in the house. I was an especially sensitive child, and I remembered the cartoon about Dumbo the elephant, and was saddened by the fact that his large ears were a subject of ridicule.

My parents constantly argued about sex, money, and power. My father was an alcoholic, selfish in his addiction. He was never honest about his whereabouts or whom he was with. He would spend money on his alcohol and on other women who would drink with him. My mother was aware of this, and would be in a rage, while my father would deny everything. When the fighting would begin, my sister and I knew to escape to our bedroom, but we still heard all that was said because the voices were so loud and heated. My mother would start to close all of the windows in the house to make sure that the neighbors wouldn't hear what was going on.

During the sixties, male privilege was the way of our society. Men were expected to make a decent salary, enough to support their wife who stayed at home with their children. If there was extra-marital activity that came with these expectations, it seemed to be part of the package. Men were expected to handle the pressure, not showing weakness, staying stoic, and carrying on. My father would often remind my mother in a rage of how much of a sacrifice he had to endure to provide the basic needs to our family. Women, on the other hand, had no rights and were expected to be submissive, making the home and motherhood their respective domains.

As the years went on and my parents' marriage deteriorated, my father would disappear in the middle of the night, sometimes staying away for days. As children, we were forbidden to question or correct adults, so we knew not to ask questions. But we also knew that he was living with another woman and her family. Living in a small town makes secrets hard to keep when everyone knows everyone else. When the fighting would start, my sister and I would retreat to our bedroom. We knew to stay out of the line of fire, since frequently both parents would grab some object and throw it to make their point. This sort of activity was much more accepted during the 1960's and 1970's and was not publically discussed.

My sister and I feared both of them and knew to always obey their rules to avoid their tempers. To comfort our mother, my sister and I would do extra chores for her, thank her for cooking us dinner, and try to make her feel like she was appreciated. We knew to never take sides in the battles but I knew from a young age that my father was deeply troubled and my mother trapped. We would hear other parents in the neighborhood outside on their porches arguing over money so I knew it was a topic that parents seemed to disagree on; it seemed almost normal to me as a young child who didn't know anything different.

I lived under a code of silence and what happened at home stayed at home. But sometimes I was allowed to play with the other children who lived on my street. I will never forget a horrible accident involving one of my neighbors. It was a weekend and I was sitting on the front steps of my parent's house on a beautiful Saturday, late in the afternoon. I heard a blood-curling scream and looked up to see eight year old Cheryl, who was one of my neighbors and my best friend, running across the street with her lower body in flames. She ran in front of a car, and the driver stopped and tried to help. Cheryl kept running to her home in search of her mother. She was the youngest of three girls who lived directly across the street from my house. I remember Cheryl's father throwing her on the family car and throwing a rug over her legs. By this time my mother had come out to the front porch and neighbors had begun to gather. I wanted to go over and comfort Cheryl, but of course my mother held me back.

The adults gathered to discuss what had gone so horribly wrong. A neighbor, who lived two doors down, a parent of four children himself, had been trying to burn an old stump from a fallen tree. He had thrown gasoline on the fire just as a strong wind came through and caused the flames to land on one of his children and on Cheryl. He tried to tackle both children but was not able. He managed to throw his child to the ground as Cheryl ran. I watched as the ambulance came and she was loaded into the cavernous vehicle. She would be gone for months to complete the required surgeries and rehabilitation work. Cheryl adjusted better than I ever could have. Seeing something so shocking at such a young age made me take fire drills seriously from that day forward; life can change in a second and I took that lesson away with me as well.

In 1966, I was in the third grade of elementary school with the tumultuous sixties raging onward. However, Jehovah's Witnesses are nonpolitical people who feel that those in Jehovah's Kingdom are not part of the world. We never discussed war in my home, because the Bible said there would be many of them in mankind's history. After the Kennedys left the White House, no one felt a need to discuss presidents. After all, no one else could have the magic that Jackie and Jack had possessed.

The most important event in third grade was getting my first pair of eyeglasses. Because I was tall, I was relegated to the back of the classroom, and was unable to see the blackboard. My teacher sent a note home to my parents, requesting that they take me to an ophthalmologist for evaluation. My vision had always been very poor; until I got glasses, I would hold a book about four inches from my face. My regular pediatrician had never checked my vision. I still remember the day those spectacles were put on my face for the very first time. Everything was so clear, crisp, and colorful! I could now see the world around me for the first time, and it enhanced my active imagination, which was a lifesaving escape for me.

During the endless hours of meetings at the Kingdom Hall my mind would wander. In my daydreams I was always male. I might be a detective on the case of the Boston strangler, or with Jules Verne under the sea. I was a young Union soldier, proudly wearing my infantry uniform into the battle of Gettysburg. I was with Jack London, desperately attempting to build a fire to keep me alive in subzero temperatures. I sailed with the pirates, looking for that buried treasure.

In my mind I could be male, as long as I never told anyone. I was always out on an adventure, far from my mother's anger and my father's alcoholism. I escaped from the small-town mentality where gossip was alive and never ending. The neighbors could be especially observant and young children would parrot adult comments. For example, a young family moved in next door to our driveway with children who were all under ten years old. Attending meetings at the Kingdom Hall meant loading the family into the car and of course, past the neighbors. As I passed by the young boy watching me getting into the car in a dress and looking as though I stepped out of a magazine, he exclaimed with shock, "I thought you were a boy! You look like a boy, act like a boy, talk like a boy, and now you look like a girl!" I could feel my mother's rage starting to build as she heard this and we silently got into the car as a family.

Nothing would anger her more than to think I was the opposite gender. She considered it a direct reflection on her and her parenting skills. She would tell me that people (who remained nameless) would speak of my sister's beauty but never mine. Her friends in the congregation could see that I was not conforming to my assigned gender and would discuss it in subtle ways. I'm sure they came up with suggestions as to how to make me appear more feminine. Perhaps a full skirt with a colorful blouse, shoes without heels so that I could take smaller steps or a pair of extremely feminine eyeglasses. No one knew what to do with a child with a nonconforming gender and so the solution was to capitalize on my feminine features, more cooking, more sewing, and raise the deep voice. My voice and my height couldn't be changed and these features were what the world saw and heard first, causing people to see me as male.

We devoted a minimum of ten hours per week to the Kingdom Hall or field service, and since my mother had been taunted because of her childhood wardrobe, mine was next to perfect. I was always in a fresh, fashionable dress or skirt, ready to go at her command. I strove for perfection in every way, to avoid her anger. She criticized me for my poor posture which was my attempt to be smaller. I walked around with a book balanced upon my head and read beauty books. Also, I knew it was a rite of passage to be asked to the adult table and to share in that cup of coffee. I was barely ten when I was allowed to sit at the adult table because I was expected to be mature and carry on an adult conversation. I was proud of this and it helped my sagging self esteem.

Because my mother had grown up in a harsh, abusive rural environment, she felt that suburban life in the 1960s was lacking structure and self-discipline. When we were not at the Kingdom Hall she assigned household chores such as dusting furniture, washing dishes, or taking the daily garbage out, since idle hands were the devil's playground. She also took us to my aunt and uncle's farm to experience the work that was needed there. Acres and acres of land needed to be plowed and planted. They had no indoor plumbing and I used the outhouse. You had to do things for yourself, because no one was going to do them for you. The farm provided us with healthy produce during every season. I watched my mother can vegetables and fruits and fill the large freezer in our basement with fresh beef from the farmer. As an adult, I realized how fortunate I was to be able to have that rural experience as a child.

Meals always included an iceberg lettuce salad that I was in charge of preparing; we never had bread or sweet desserts. My mother always declared she was already too heavy and did not need the extra calories from baked goods. I never appreciated the meals that I had as a child until I became an adult, when I was surprised to hear of childhood meals consisting of frozen and canned food.

In 1966, Frederick Franz, vice president of the Watchtower Bible and Tract Society authored the book *Life Everlasting in Freedom of the Sons of God.* This book was released at the assembly of Jehovah's Witnesses on June 22, 1966, and I was in attendance. It was the first to announce that 1975 was the target date for Armageddon. Mr. Franz came to this date by his research, which stated that man's creation date was 4026 B.C.E. According to Bible chronology, 6000 years of man's creation would end in 1975. The seventh period of human history would begin in the fall of 1975 C.E. Before this "seventh day" could begin, God would destroy Satan at Armageddon. The end of the sixth creative day could end with the same Gregorian calendar year of Adam's creation.

I was to graduate from high school in 1976, and this belief haunted me for decades. As an adult I would struggle with nightmares of what was supposed to happen but did not. However, at the time I was only ten years old and forced to think of the upcoming apocalypse where I was told I would be housed in a concentration camp because I was a conscientious objector. Furthermore, preparation for this apocalypse may involve the loss of my life since there would be another major world war worse than the Second World War. Of course, as a ten year old child who would listen to the adults discuss this horror, I believed it to be true. I was not a true believer in all scriptural doctrines that I was taught, but this one I did believe. The sixties were a turbulent decade with one horrific event after another that we had never seen before. It was effortless to connect one dot of revolution to another dot of assassination to a final dot of ongoing war to see Jehovah's influence in all that was happening. The only preparation the adults spoke of was going underground at a moment's notice.

In 1967, I entered the fourth grade, moving up to the second floor of my school building, another rite of passage as the upper grades were on the second floor. The Vietnam War was going at full steam during those years, although my parents never discussed it. At home, thousands of anti-war protesters demonstrated throughout the nation. Anti-draft rallies were held in Chicago, Philadelphia, Boston, Cincinnati and Portland. Young men set draft cards on fire at churches and federal offices. All of these events were considered biblical prophecy. Each time a new event would occur there would soon be a discussion at the Kingdom Hall explaining how we were in the midst of "the last days."

My life changed in 1967, when I started menstruating. I did not know how to tell my mother, and she found out by accident when she laundered my clothes for the week. I was so shocked that this plunge into the depths of womanhood had happened so quickly. As a class, our teachers separated us by gender to view the boring movie on starting to menstruate. It was awkward because no one knew what to do and we got in trouble if we snickered. So we silently watched the movie and took home a booklet for our parents. My mother had filled me in on things and I just felt so sad; I wasn't prepared for it. I hated the horrible cramps and the bulky Kotex and the disgusting sanitary belt that kept it in place. I wept, and at the same time, was angry.

I did not want children; I didn't even want to be a girl. At school, I was still the tallest person in my class, towering at five feet eight inches at ten years old. In every class photo I was at the very top of the pyramid. In addition, I now had recess with fourth and fifth graders. They called me "Lurch," after the character from the popular television series *The Addams Family*. Not only was I the tallest person in the class, but I also had that ever-present deep voice that made me sound male. Kinder nicknames for me were "Stringbean" and "Jolly Green Giant."

I dreaded recess and running from the bullies; I was always afraid, humiliated and embarrassed.

With the onset of puberty and hormones came rebellion and a greater sense of self awareness. For the first time, at age ten, I put on a pair of blue jeans and a man's shirt. I felt powerful as I put them on, and could not stop looking at myself in the mirror. I felt as if the inside of me matched the outside of me and I was in the appropriate clothing where I belonged. On the rare occasions when I was alone in the house, I would try on my father's neckties and suit coats. This was when I would feel the most powerful: in the corporate male uniform. My father was meticulous in his appearance, almost a bit of a dandy. All clothing, ties, belt and shoes would match. I wanted to dress this way and I would always make a mental note of what colors he would wear with what color of shoes. I would head to the public library under the guise of studying to search the stacks in an attempt to understand what was wrong with me. Why was I inside a body that was not mine?

Very little printed information was available at the time, and what did exist was to be found in the "deviant psychology" part of the Reference section of the library. Since no language existed at this time except "transvestite" which I had not heard yet, I thought I must be gay. After all, gay people wear clothes of the opposite gender and strive to be the opposite gender so that must be who I am. Homosexuality was considered to be a mental illness until 1973, when I was a sophomore in high school. Only then did the American Psychiatric Association delete homosexuality from its diagnostic handbook. I had heard the word somewhere in the schoolyard but had no idea what it meant. I looked up the definition alone and secretly. I wrote it down on lined notebook paper and stored it in my coat pocket, because I wanted to read it again.

My mother always searched my clothes, and of course she found that paper in my coat pocket. She flew into a rage, demanding to know why I would have that word in my possession. I told her an older student at school had uttered the word, and I was trying to learn what it meant. She knew that I was lying, and she was furious. She struck me across my face with a lightning-fast backhand. I had no doubt that as a parent she knew what I could not dare say. I felt as though I had done something dirty and wrong just by writing the word with the definition. The word "homosexuality" would later be used in our house and always followed up with disgust and contempt, especially by my father. I grew up during a time when mothers frequently blamed themselves for their children's imperfections, with my mother feeling especially responsible for a child who would not conform to set gender standards.

I became more guarded at home, and she became more determined to control me. I also began to resent her religion controlling my life, as she became more determined to beat it into me. The seeds of my double life were being planted. At home, I would act the way I had to around her to avoid punishment. At school it was my time to be with my friends and teachers. I had a supportive group of friends and teachers who were there for me.

With puberty, the question arose that I would be asked throughout my entire life by strangers: "Are you a boy or a girl?" I would try to sense that it was about to happen, and avoid the situation. I could see it with someone who had just walked past me and looked puzzled. Someone in a department store might point at me and snicker. After all, we must know a person's gender before we communicate or have any interaction with them. If there is any question in the gender appearance, that becomes the time to bully or laugh at that person.

FIVE

During my elementary school years, I saw some excellent movies that had a lasting effect on me. I saw them on a large screen in a theater that showed only one movie, not the fifteen chopped up theaters that we have today.

I saw *Gone With The Wind* at that impressionable age and wept at the horrors of the Civil War. After that, I read everything I could about The Civil War. In *Romeo and Juliet* I saw what hatred and prejudice can do to a society. That theme was repeated in *West Side Story*. When I saw *The Sound of Music* it sparked my interest in Nazi Germany.

By the time I finished fourth grade in 1968, the country had taken a horrible turn to violence and murder. Senator Robert F. Kennedy of New York announced his candidacy for president on March 16. Dr. Martin Luther King Junior was assassinated in Memphis on April 4. King's murder enraged the nation's African-American communities. Chicago, Baltimore, Washington and Cincinnati were the hardest hit by arson, looting, and violence. Robert Kennedy attended Dr. King's funeral; however, he too would be assassinated in Los Angeles on June 5th. I arrived at school on that day to complete silence in the classrooms, as well as the halls. I could see that my teacher, Mrs. Murphy, was extremely upset. My principal played the radio news throughout the entire school via the public address system. We listened to the news as it happened that day, and my class was very attentive. The nation had lost two very powerful leaders within the span of three months. We watched the funeral of another Kennedy, gunned down in violence.

The Olympics were held in Mexico that year, and I remember my mother gasping as Tommy Smith and John

Carlos, first and third in the 200-meter track event, accepted their medals. They wore black scarves and black gloves and raised their clenched fists in the Black Power salute during the playing of the National Anthem. They were suspended from the Games and expelled from the Olympic Village for using the victory celebration as a black power organizing tool.

One of the most important aspects of being one of Jehovah's Witnesses was the ever-present Bible study, not just within the family unit, but with those who expressed interest in the religion. This was needed to bring recruits into the organization and was considered to be an important activity. I would travel with my parents to the home of the interested party and study a publication specifically designed to recruit people into the organization. These publications involved a question-and-answer discussion about the principles and rules of becoming one of Jehovah's Witnesses. There was a discussion of scriptural doctrines that would aid in the understanding of what Jehovah's Witnesses believed.

These Bible studies were with people from all walks of life. The congregation that I grew up in was very diverse and included Hispanics, African-Americans and even Canadians. My mother studied the Bible with a Hispanic family of migrant workers who lived in extreme poverty. Their housing consisted of a double car garage with a curtain pulled down the center. A bare light bulb hung from the center of the ceiling, and a pie tin with a hole poked through the center was used as a lamp shade. Sometimes I would watch the small mouse that would come out of the woodwork because it was so quiet. There was little furniture, only beds and a table and chairs. The ten children slept on one side of the curtain and the two adults slept on the other side. I went with my mother to buy toys and clothing for the children and she taught me a valuable life lesson: to always help others. She had the means to do this and never once hesitated; in fact, she considered it her duty simply because she was in the position to do so. I did not know this at the time, but within the next twenty years I would take this lesson to heart and never look back. I only knew I had a responsibility to share my resources with others.

I was fortunate enough at ten years old to have a great-grandmother who was still alive. She ran a secondhand store out of her home. The store was in the front of the house and she lived in the back of the house. The shop was located in the large rooms of an older home. My mother would take all of the family's clothing there to be resold and recycled once we outgrew them. How I loved to go shop there! I would escape to the second floor of the house, and try on football uniforms, boy's shoes and clothes. Shopping there was always an adventure, and one that fed my imagination. My great-grandmother was well into her eighties, yet very active and alert. This was in sharp contrast to my grandmother who lived in complete rural poverty. When I asked my mother about the contrast between the two women, she told me that my grandmother was the black sheep of the family. She had planned to attend college and study journalism, but like many of life's best prepared plans; it did not work out that way. She married an abusive husband, had four children and was unable to get out of the all encompassing poverty cycle. Her siblings had a much better life, and there was a huge gulf between them. I was much more attentive about those kinds of things as I was getting older and able to see the differences in people's lives.

SIX

I started fifth grade with a wonderful young teacher who insisted on making her classroom both fun and exciting. She insisted that we participate in the "duck walk" one morning and I remember it being hard for me to lower my long legs into that squatting position. If that were not bad enough, I then ripped out the entire hem on the skirt I was wearing. Oh, the joy of being the tallest and most awkward girl in the class! My mother was not happy when I came home with my story, and of course I was told that this is what happened when I walked like a boy. It was during this time that I became daring and went over to the neighbor's house to visit a family who had two beautiful girls, both older than me. The oldest of the girls was wearing the pale pink lipstick that was so popular that year. I knew that because my mother wore that same shade. I waited until I was alone with her and I was only able to see those pink lips through my tunnel vision. I took her face into my hands, planted a kiss on those pink lips and said, "What would you do if I told you that I was not a girl at all but was really a boy?" I thought it was a fair enough question, but she went running into the house, and of course her mother called my mother on the phone and I was not allowed to play with either of the girls any more. My mother was furious that I had done this and I was punished. It was, however, the first time I had said what had always been inside my head. I knew not to speak of it again to anyone.

When I entered sixth grade, I had a male teacher; he was from Canada, and very soft spoken: an outstanding teacher. I authored my first poem in sixth grade, and on my report card he instructed my mother to encourage creative writing at home. We read Jack London and discussed it as a class, and because I was still at home sick a third of the school year, he worked with me individually to catch me up on the elementary geometry that was being introduced as part of the math curriculum. I had gone from getting A's in math down to a B and would continue to decline in the upcoming years. All of the time that I had missed was catching up with me, and I was not bouncing back on the missed material like I had in previous years.

My teacher was devoted to classroom discussions and the current events of that school year were ones that I will always remember. For example, he brought in the *Life* magazine that showed pictures of the My Lai massacre. Lt. Calley Jr. was being charged with the murder of the civilians involved. The country was able to see the horrors of the Vietnam War from their sofas and on their televisions. As I matured, I was able to understand how horrific the war was, especially the death toll.

We landed on the moon that year and produced The Woodstock Music and Art Festival in New York State. I was fascinated with Woodstock and still own the two sets of triple albums that were released containing the powerful music of that magical event. I also shared a hospital room with a woman who had attended. Talking to her about Woodstock was one of the high points of my life because I really wanted to be old enough to be there. I wanted to have ten years added to my life so instead of only being eleven, I could be twenty-one. I wanted to be involved in the anti-war movement, the war on poverty movement, the civil rights movement. I wanted to be a part of the history that was changing the country at the time.

There was another historical event that happened in 1969 that I continue to celebrate today but was unaware of when it actually happened. In New York City, at a Greenwich Village gay bar called the Stonewall Inn, New York City police had enforced yet another raid on a late Saturday night in June. This was standard practice, and during that time in history, any male wearing three articles of women's clothing could be arrested since it was against the law. Many clubs had shows that starred female impersonators who were called "drag queens." They would entertain patrons by impersonating Judy Garland, Marilyn Monroe and the other great female entertainers. As the police entered the bar ready to make arrests, the drag queens, who were wearing women's clothing, attacked them and a full scale riot ensued, first in the bar and then out into the street. That marked the beginning of the Gay Liberation Movement, when gays in America decided that they were going to fight back. I celebrate this anniversary every year with pride.

We began the 1970's which would be memorable to me personally for different reasons than the rest of the world. After all, Armageddon was scheduled to begin in the fall of 1975. There was no real concrete data from the Watchtower Bible and Tract Society concerning the logistics of the battle. This allowed for various impending doomsday scenarios on the part of all concerned. An elder would announce at the international assembly of Jehovah's Witnesses in the summer of 1970 that we were entering the "shaky seventies," thus setting the stage for the collective hysteria that would follow. There was a theory that all Jehovah's Witnesses would go into an underground movement. I overheard my mother, lamenting the fact that my sister and I were in two different school buildings and thus it would take another step to whisk both of us away on a moment's notice. There was increased discussion during Bible study that there would be concentration camps just as there were during the Second World War. There were Jehovah's Witnesses who were executed then, and this fact has been historically established. In fact, they were issued purple triangles.

I would see that graphic symbol while in Washington DC, in the neighborhood of DuPont Circle while in a gay bookstore. The mere sight of that symbol took my breath away, and I realized that The Society was right about this historical content, and this was not just more propaganda.

Of course, I had *The Diary of Anne Frank*, while in junior high school, thinking that this would be my life as well. I eventually saw the movie and will always remember the last of the dialogue when the Gestapo breaks the door down and it is finally over. For years, all of them had lived in fear and now they would live in hope. I was unable to see the hope, because I was unable to get past the fear. My mother explained to me that an execution by firing squad would not hurt, and it would be over quickly. I envisioned first digging my grave, as so many prisoners were required to do before that final act.

I was instructed to never, ever question any order that was given to me by either my parents or the elders in my congregation, because my life might depend upon following those orders. Another elder would profess from the pulpit that as a congregation, if we were on the shores of The Great Lakes region with nothing but the clothes upon our back it would be the best that we could hope for. Yet another elder stated that we would simply close our drapes and let Jehovah battle Satan with no further prophecy than that. The push began to make a direct correlation between current events and Bible prophecy. Religions have done this since the beginning of time. At any given minute, there are earthquakes, floods and famines in numerous places throughout the world. There is endless minutiae and fodder to fuel the doomsday theories. I purchased my high school class ring, which had my graduation date of 1976 stamped in bold numbers on the side. A sister in my congregation saw it and reminded me that I would never graduate because the world as we know it would not last until then.

During this time the emergency services vehicles had changed the tone of their sirens. What seemed to be a curious change in tone scared me to the point of running up to my bedroom in an attempt to hide. I thought that the new tone of the sirens meant that just like Anne Frank, my time had come to be captured and to live in fear. I thought these new sirens belonged to a group of military police ready to take me into custody because I did not salute the flag nor would agree to active military service.

Jehovah's Witnesses took a very passive, non-political stance in the battle of Armageddon. There was the philosophy that it was unavoidable, and the best preparation was to remain strong in your loyalty to Jehovah. Death was never to be feared, and there were no teachings of heaven or hell. Death was to be a prolonged peaceful sleep until the resurrection took place. There was no stockpiling of food or weapons, no active resistance against those who persecute you. Instead, many brothers, in anticipation of this biblical battle, quit their jobs, liquidated all of their assets including their homes, and spent as much time as possible trying to save others. My father, despite his double life, decided to retire early and devote more time to God's Kingdom, a way to redeem himself I am sure, always the addict and always self-centered in his actions, thinking only of his own skin. He cashed in his entire retirement when the markets were at their lowest because of the resignation of President Nixon.

As the systematic psychological hysteria mounted during the 1970s, the number of active Jehovah's Witnesses increased by 20% to 1.5 million in August of 1971. By 1974, there was another increase of 13.5%. Later, as an adult, I looked back on this timeline, trying to make sense of the fact that none of it had happened. However, at the time that all of this was happening, I was only beginning the seventh grade in junior high school and I believed that I was going to die and prepared myself for that as best as I could.

The spring of 1970 found me sitting on the sun porch of my childhood home, reading *Life* magazine. My mother had arranged for *Life* magazine and *National Geographic* magazine to be delivered to the house for years. I treasured reading these beloved periodicals as they were my connection to the outside world, away from the constant dogma of Jehovah's organization. I remember reading the issue of *Life* magazine that covered the May 4, 1970 killings at Kent State University. In fact, I still have that issue in my archives today as one of my many collections of history. As I read that issue, I made a promise to myself that if I lived, I was going to attend that university. By this time, I knew I would always have to support myself because I knew I wanted nothing to do with heterosexual marriage. I pictured myself as unmarried and needing an income so that I would never have to depend on anyone to support me. I wanted nothing to do with the life I saw my parents living: fighting over money, power and sex; filled with destruction at every disastrous turn.

In the summer of 1970 I visited New York City for the very first time. I was there, of course, for an assembly of Jehovah's Witnesses in Yankee Stadium. There were over 100,000 people attending the event, and logistics involving meals, transportation and bathrooms were complicated. The bathroom lines were endless and since my mother would forbid me to use the bathroom except during the lunch and dinner hour, I was constantly worried I would not be able to go that long without being extremely uncomfortable. In fact, inside the women's bathrooms, the mirrors were taped off with butcher block paper with the inscription: "Jehovah does not care about your outward beauty only your spiritual beauty." Because the crowds were so large and it took so long to feed everyone, meals consisted of cold lunch meat sandwiches and a piece of fruit. Sessions began at 9 A.M. and went on until 9 P.M. Monday through Sunday.

Keeping with my mother's tradition, a few days were spent sightseeing in the city before the assembly began. I was able to see the Empire State Building, the Statue of Liberty and Rockefeller Center. What I cherished the most was going to a restaurant and seeing native New Yorkers combined with the contrast between the culture of my one-horse town and one of the largest cities in the world. For the first time ever, I saw women not wearing a bra and I had to look twice. I also saw men eating together who seemed to be more than just buddies. Even at my tender age I was able to pick up on the fact that they were different and different like me. Long hair on men was the style then, and I always noticed when there were two men together, one with long hair and more effeminate than the other.

It was at that time that I realized there were others who were like me in the world. Despite my sheltered existence and warped knowledge of the world, this was the beginning of me taking in cultures that were unfamiliar to me. I silently rejoiced, never once displaying my newly found secret. Actually, I grew up quite a bit on that two week trip with all that I experienced. In order to get to Yankee Stadium we were required to take the subway, which was a first in my young life. The subways were loud, dirty and very crowded especially in the early morning hours. I always looked and acted far more mature than my years with no one realizing my actual age.

One morning, while on an extremely crowded car, I felt the presence of the man behind me. He was not much taller than I was, briefcase in hand, wearing a suit on his morning commute. He wore very dark sunglasses, and his face was pitted showing the scars of an acne induced puberty. Before I realized what was happening, I was able to feel his full erection tenting through his slacks and up against my buttocks. I was horrified and stomped on his foot that was so close to mine, hoping to stop his actions but to no avail. I tried to shift positions and move away from him, but as I did this my mother saw me and told me that we were not ready to exit at the next stop and to stay put. Finally, I turned and glared at him, hoping that my silent confrontation would cause him to stop. Nothing worked, and I spent the entire time afraid, embarrassed and ashamed that this was happening to me.

SEVEN

As an adult, I have no doubt that the conventions of Jehovah's Witnesses attracted those men who were predators, since Jehovah's Witnesses were known for their naïveté and isolation from the general population. No sooner had I reached Yankee Stadium before another man, slightly shorter than I but with no glasses, was behind me and running his hand over my bare thigh. I would not wear nylon stockings for another four years, so my legs were bare, except for bobby socks with loafers. Once again I attempted to step on feet, walk faster, glare and stare to escape this menace. The crowds were almost unbearable; walking was difficult and slow, because there were just so many people. As the week wore on, more and more people would fill the stands of the stadium, until the weekend and the highest attendance of the entire week when everyone would be grappling for seats.

The days were long, hot, and dirty, with each day beginning by seven in the morning and not ending until 10 o'clock at night by the time we hit the crowded subways to the hotel. Because there were such large crowds, exiting the stadium was a long ordeal. In the mornings, we needed to arrive early for a seat in the shade. It seemed to be exceptionally hot and exhausting that summer when dealing with the intensity of one of the largest cities in the world.

Also included in that hot summer in New York City was a visit by a group of individuals who had once been active in the Watchtower Bible and Tract Society, but had since departed and were now back in "the world." They would form a picket line, timed to greet all those who exited the stadium, and pass out literature that described the religion as a dangerous cult. I was ordered to lower my head and not even look at them as we passed on the way to the subway. This was a first for me, as I had never had exposure to someone who had left the organization and talked about the ordeal.

This yearly pilgrimage to various cities, from Chicago to Pittsburgh to New York City, was as much a part of my life as attending public school. We always drove, as flying would have been cost prohibitive. Had I not developed the art of daydreaming and escaping the endless hours of boredom I would not have survived. I read the license plates of cars passing me, learning all of the states. I read books, and did anything I could think of to make the time go faster.

I also daydreamed by the hour that I was male, even though I was unable to show it on the outside. I was forced to dress the way that my mother instructed and I was miserable. What was in my mind and the way that I thought of myself was never reflected to anyone, although people certainly were confused by my female presentation. Every place that I went would bring stares, snickering and pointing. I was too tall, my voice too deep, my gait too wide to resemble the average female. I knew it and the rest of the world knew it as well. I tried to wear clothes that had a hint of a classic style: penny loafers, blouses and skirts, but nothing helped.

With that New York City trip still fresh in my memory, in December of 1970, we headed to Phoenix and the southwest to visit my father's side of the family. Many of them, I had seen only once or twice in my life and some never at all. Utilizing thrift at every turn, we took a red-eye flight and changed planes, complete with a layover in Dallas. It was my first time ever on a plane, and it felt like a rocket ship. The take-off caused my guts to fly into my throat and my ears hurt down to my jaw line. Nothing helped the ear pain, not yawning for six hours or chewing gum. When I finally arrived at Scottsdale's Sky Harbor Airport, I thought I was in a different country since nothing was like what I had left behind. Not the landscape, the fashion or the architecture. There were cowboys, tacos and avocados, ranch houses with pebbles in the front yards instead of green grass. Mountains that touched the sky. full of brown and red hues with some green dotting the hills.

I met cousins that I did not know I had, who were also Jehovah's Witnesses. In fact, all of my father's family was active in my childhood religion, making it easy to stay for weeks at a time in the southwest and still attend all meetings. We simply accompanied the family to their congregation for the time we were there.

I had a second cousin named Joe who actually looked like a brother to my father, middle aged and obese. He had a wife and three children and was a successful, self-made businessman. Although he was quick tempered, he married a woman who would simmer his temper. They had relocated to Phoenix decades earlier, when the city was smaller, and he installed drywall in the new construction. As the city grew, his business grew until he had his own company with employees. He and his family were at the point in their lives where they were enjoying all of the material trappings of the fruits of his labor. There were two new Cadillacs in the driveway next to a huge ranch home. There was a gigantic custom built camper on a two ton pickup truck that housed five people comfortably. The back yard had a built-in pool complete with orange trees lining the perimeter of the property. I will never forget the thrill of going into that back yard, taking a swim and then picking my first orange off of a tree.

My cousin Joe appeared as though the world was his in 1970. He enjoyed throwing money around and enjoyed a childlike fun in all that he did. His addiction was not alcohol but food. All was centered on the next meal: at breakfast there was a discussion of lunch, at lunch there was a discussion of dinner. Joe and his family traveled the entire summer, up and down the coast of California, visiting the same top quality restaurants and sites along the way. The staff and owners of all the restaurants knew him by name and no matter how many people were in line, he would be given preferential treatment.

Money talks in a capitalistic society and he had what seemed to be an endless supply.

I accompanied his family on the trip of a lifetime, beginning in Phoenix and ending in beautiful San Francisco. It was a first for me and very memorable, with our party of nine traveling in both the camper and the Cadillac. My parents, my sister and I started our trip to California alone in the Cadillac, and met up with Joe and his family after crossing the desert after nightfall. There was a darkness that enveloped the desert that was thick, humid, and as black as coal. Not even so much as a star or sliver of moon was in the nighttime sky. There was only a lonely two-lane highway with no other cars in sight.

Suddenly, out of nowhere up ahead in the distance, laid a body draped, motionless, just over the double yellow line on the highway. It was a young white male with no sight of blood or trauma. It was as though he had been hitchhiking and had been clipped by a passing vehicle, with his right arm still outstretched on the pavement. He looked surreal, as if my eyes were playing a trick on me. My mother screamed at my father that there was a body in the road and he swerved at the last minute to avoid hitting the body. I was riding in the back seat of a 1970 Cadillac, my heart pounding through my chest, just seconds ago asleep but now wide awake. My parents debated how to handle the situation and decided that they would pull off at the next available exit and phone the police. When I tried to sleep that night I was plagued with nightmares playing out the scenario as a set up for a gang robbery. A car would stop to check on the body and a gang of robbers would appear from the tumbleweed, guns drawn, demanding money and jewelry. Who knows if what happened that night was a staged robbery waiting to be played out? Was the body placed there from another location already deceased? Was it a hit-and-run accident that had just happened maybe hours ago?

When speaking to my relatives about the incident the next day, they were much calmer about the whole situation, making me realize once again, the difference between a small town and a major city. Should something like that happen in my small town it would be headline news; however, in a larger city it simply wasn't that big of a deal. An accident of this nature would happen on a much more frequent basis and may or may not involve foul play. However, I was immersed in the human factor, thinking of what might have happened and concerned for the victim involved.

As the trip continued, I traveled in both the Cadillac and the custom camper, switching off throughout the long drive from Phoenix into Los Angeles. I was in the camper when we approached the lights of Los Angeles during the Christmas season of 1970. I will never forget that scene: so many lights as far as the eye could see; it was a first for me. While in New York City, I had never seen the display of lights over the shoreline because it was a working vacation, and once I hit the hotel I was ready to sleep. The sites that we did see were visited during the day, but the trip to the West Coast was different and there would be time for play. While in Los Angeles, I was able to see all of the tourist sites including Sunset Boulevard, Universal Studios, and Sid Gram's Chinese Theater.

After a week in Los Angeles I was on the road again with my relatives and family, driving up the coast of California in all of its splendor and beauty. The views were breathtaking once we left the confines of the city's boundaries. We proceeded due north up the coast on beautiful Highway One with the eventual goal of ending up in San Francisco. I saw Chinatown, Disneyland, Sea World, Busch Gardens and San Simeon, the beautiful Hearst mansion. Out of a fairy tale, the structure was difficult to grasp as being in reality. There was beauty everywhere I looked. Clark Gable and Vivian Leigh viewed the movie *Gone With The Wind* there as guests of the tycoon-millionaire William Randolph Hearst. The history that took place in that mansion was so immense it was hard to take it all in during one visit.

Disneyland was a true fantasy, just like the movies and the image that Walt had always given us on television. I felt nausea on the Mad Hatter tea cup ride and fear as I rode the Matterhorn, but mostly I tried to comprehend the vastness of that kingdom. I still own the trademark sweatshirt I bought during that visit and I always smile whenever I see it. Disneyland is truly a fantasy world for children that the adults share in as well.

Sea World and Busch Gardens maintained their own beauty, although on a smaller scale, and I enjoyed all of it immensely. Because there was so much to do, conversation was easier and more about the activity that was planned for that day. No one in my traveling party took the time to read the newspaper or even listen to the news. After all, everyone was a member of the Watchtower Bible and Tract Society, a separatist organization. Current events were not discussed except in scriptural context. Nothing was said about the soldiers and sailors who were on holiday leave and attending the same amusement parks. When I think back on things, there was so much history that was made during 1970; we were still fighting the Vietnam War. We saw the troops coming home on holiday leave at the airports. Once my mother made a comment that she knew it was a sister who came to greet a soldier because they looked alike. On the other hand, I could feel the happiness within that family of seeing their child still alive while others were fighting in a horrible endless war.

My favorite city was San Francisco, with the hippies in the Haight-Asbury district and the smell of Fisherman's Wharf alive with tourists. It was magical without the high stress of Los Angeles, the air cleaner and people more relaxed. In addition to the tourist traps, we spent a lot of time touring museums. There was a huge museum in the city where our entourage spent the afternoon. I enjoyed any sort of culture, since my one-horse town had very little of it. I also had a passion for black and white photographs and was drawn to a section of the museum that had a group of them assembled together in an orderly fashion. At first glance, it appeared to be a voyeuristic look into the lives of people at a wedding in progress. The bride and groom were both standing next to their wedding cake, each holding a glass of champagne in a silent toast captured by the camera. The bride wore beautiful white gloves up to her elbows, and completed the look-of-the-day with a white netted veil that was flowing back away from her face and perched on the back of her head. As I studied the photo I felt there was something different about it, but I was unsure as to exactly what that was. As I continued to silently scrutinize the subjects, I was finally able to see that the balance of the two individuals was different. The heads were large and the noses were larger than what appeared to be normal. As I continued silently studying, it finally occurred to me that the two individuals in the photograph were both male. The Mapplethorpe-esque exhibit consisted of photographs from the gay community in a gay wedding ceremony. I didn't want to stop looking for fear that they would disappear forever, so I stood there soaking up every last detail, silently rejoicing to myself that there were other people like me in the world. I had a beautiful photograph in front of me to prove it!

All of a sudden I could hear the thunderous voice of my cousin Joe behind me, "I can't believe they're showing something as disgusting as homosexuals in a museum and calling it art! I'm going to tell them how disgusting this is, especially when I paid money to come in here with my wife and children!" I turned to see Joe running in a full rage, his face beet red, the veins in his thick, oversized neck bulging, with my father running after him and chiming in so as to show his approval of this public demonstration. Of course we would all need to leave immediately; otherwise we may be turned into a pillar of salt. My mother, ever willing to show my father how little attention he paid to his children, replied in seething sarcasm, "You're a little late; your daughter has seen the entire exhibit. Where were you all this time?" I remained silent and emotionless, trying to stay out of the line of fire. Inside I was screaming with joy but stoic on the outside. Between New York City and now San Francisco, I had seen people who were like me; they weren't heterosexual like everyone I had ever met, but dressed as if they were born in the opposite birth gender. Experiencing this brought me untold joy and the feelings that I wasn't insane. I knew that I was different, but I had no one to voice these feelings to, and thus thought that I was alone in the world. I kept my thoughts and feelings to myself but after the two trips to both coasts within a year's time, I knew that I was not alone and that thought comforted me for years to come.

EIGHT

I started junior high school in the fall of 1970. Just as the turbulent decade of the sixties had come to an end and the country began a new chapter, my life began a new chapter as well. All was different in junior high than what I had been accustomed to: although I still was able to walk to school, I now had a different teacher for every subject. Also, social clubs, sports and extra-curricular activities shaped the landscape of the school day. I was forbidden to participate in any of these functions, so by default I ended up in a gang of other girls who were also not part of any extra-curricular activities. I spent grades seven through nine in an older building, where the blackboards were black instead of green, and the desks were bolted into the floor of our huge classrooms. The floors were hardwood and polished to a beautiful shine. The ceilings were high and painted a bright white. The entrance to our building was brick with beautiful white pillars that would flank the doors.

My teachers were young and progressive, dedicated and loyal to the student body. They were kind to me and were always there to talk or assist me through those difficult times that seemed never ending.

Things changed for me when I went into junior high, and I became rebellious in every way. I was making a new set of friends for the first time, since my junior high combined all of the outlying elementary schools. I was painfully aware of how much free time my classmates had for other activities, and I was tired of spending so much of my time in my religious faith.

My mother was determined to keep me in line with discipline, and punishments escalated during those years. Her rage felt terrifying to me, and I never knew when or what would start the rapid ascent. Raising any child is difficult; however, I'm sure my mother had no idea what to do with me and my unique chemistry. Not only was I rebelling against my religious upbringing, but also rebelling against being female and society in general. My newly formed gang of girls, who understood me, allowed me for the first time to shift my loyalty away from anything but my peers and my teachers. My gang of girls, also on the fringe of school life, were understanding and loyal. We shared endless laughter and sophomoric jokes and pranks throughout our three years together. It would be the last time that I would be with the same group of friends for three consecutive years while in public school.

Life with my parents was slowly imploding on every front. My father's alcoholism was getting worse every year. He was spending more and more time away from my mother, instead, with his "other family." My parent's marriage continued to deteriorate as the fighting escalated, putting my sister and me in our silent bedroom, lying silently and fearfully on our twin beds more and more often. The pressure of 1975 and Armageddon arriving was also looming over us. No one spoke of how it would happen, only that it would arrive without fail. Members would speak of how there were only five years left; the Watchtower Bible and Tract Society would spend more and more time instructing us to save more people from the impending deadline

The more that I rebelled, the more energy I put in to cover my tracks to avoid being punished. I was going through the average physical and social child development into my teenage years; however, this average development was never allowed in Jehovah's Witnesses' youths. During this time you were to mature into young adults ready to serve Jehovah without going through any sort of teenage development. This put the pressure on my mother to forbid any normal sort of development and thus normal behavior of a teenager trying to find their place in the world. Instead, she was more determined than ever to control me and get me into Jehovah's kingdom within the next five years. On the other hand, I would spend the next five years in a nonstop state of fear, always waiting for Armageddon to arrive and hyper-vigilant in watching for any signs of it on the horizon.

As early as seventh grade, things were changing, with my grades in math and science coming down to average and below. All through grade school, my grades had been above average, but all the time that I was absent due to illness was starting to catch up with me. I had missed so much of the learning that took place in those early elementary years. Science and math were not as interesting to me as history and English literature; history and literature books filled every bookcase in my bedroom. Instead of seeking help, I developed an attitude of not caring. In my junior high school, most of my math and science teachers were men. In an effort to save money, a male teacher could be hired by day to teach math or science and be a coach by afternoon, supplying the other needed component to public education: sports. My teachers in English and history were usually young women whom I adored. I would work harder in their classes because I enjoyed them and the subject matter. At the end of the grading period my grades would run the extremes of A's to D's, depending on the subject.

Math was most difficult for me, and with each year it became more and more difficult. By my freshman year I was placed in Pre-Algebra with a teacher who was the male basketball coach and would arrange the seating chart of the class by test score. In other words, students who received the highest scores would sit in the front seats with the next highest scores in the seats behind that. By the time I was given a seat according to my test score, I was in the second to the last seat in the classroom. In fact, a fellow student named Keith and I always occupied those last two seats. After one test I would sit in that last seat, and after another test, he would sit in that last seat. I remained there the entire school year and missed passing the class by one failing grade. Yet, my next class period had me attending an advanced placement history class in which I earned the highest grades with minimal effort. This was the beginning of extremes in my life, traveling from one end of the spectrum to the other within one day. This pattern became a staple in my life well into adulthood.

Junior high school also brought segregated physical education classes along with required jump suit uniforms. For me, it was the dreaded gym class that would require showering in front of my classmates. Once again, I went from one extreme to the other, with humiliation thrown in for shameful measure. Some sports like archery and soccer I was able to excel in; I was able to run and kick a ball on the ground, and I had played with a backyard archery set as a child. Soccer was brutal, as my classmates seemed to always hit my shins rather than the ball and shin guards were nonexistent. I would go home with bruises from my knees to my feet but never once during the game let on that I was in horrible pain. Beyond those two sports, gym class was a nightmare. I was unable to tumble or swing on the parallel bars, much less balance on the balance beam. I was far too uncoordinated; instead I would try and "spot" a classmate who excelled in twirling around the dreaded bars. Volleyball was almost impossible because I didn't do well with a ball being thrown at my face. Basketball, a sport that everyone thought I should be able to play with ease because I was so tall, was the biggest misconception. I was unable to dribble and run at the same time, much less dribble, run, and shoot a basket correctly. During the early 1970's in my junior high, the gym teacher would pick two girls, who then picked two teams to face off in a game. This was especially humiliating. The anxiety would begin as I would wonder when I would be chosen. Popularity was part of the equation; friends were picked first, others were then chosen by ability to play. I would finally be picked at the second half of the draft but felt so bad for the girls who were left standing at the end, to be shuffled in as an afterthought. In 1975, the folk singer Janis Ian described the agony of gym class and being the last picked for basketball in her song, "At Seventeen." Years later, I purchased the album, grateful that someone understood my plight and was able to so eloquently describe it. Decades later, Janis Ian would publicly come out as a lesbian.

Softball was the worst of the entire physical education curriculum. I could neither hit nor catch the fat white ball. Running was a secondary skill behind the eye-hand coordination required for the game. When it was my turn to head into the field I would go to the farthest part of the outfield and hide from the ball. When up to bat, I invariably struck out, causing more humiliation and feelings of failure.

The very end of gym class would bring the dreaded shower that no one wanted to take, but it was required as part of our earned grade. We were excused from showering if we were menstruating, which we were to announce to the gym teacher with (it always seemed) the rest of the class. The gym teacher would appear by our lockers, class roster and pencil in hand, asking who was and was not taking a shower. If we were menstruating, we were to state the one word that released us from the dreaded task: "regular." However, in private with junior high sophomoric behavior, we referred to the term as "rag." This was a standing joke with all of my peers at the time so when the gym teacher came around, we would usually slip up and start to say the word "rag" instead of the allowed term of "regular." So in speaking to the stern gym teacher peering over our shoulder, the word usually came out as "ragular!" There would then be snickering and smirks throughout my peer group as my gym teacher would get red faced and reply, "Pardon me?" I would have a period once every three weeks, but when it came to showering in that steamy locker room, I would have a period whenever possible. It was fashionable during those years to wear nylon stockings and even girdles with skirts and dresses. There was never enough time to completely dry before the bell would summon us to our next class, so when I did have to shower, I would attempt to put nylon stockings over my wet legs which never worked.

During the junior high years, the sophomoric humor is never ending and I'm proud to say that my classmates and I carried on that tradition. There were various items that were contraband and if seen would be confiscated. One of these items was what we referred to as "slam books." They consisted of a spiral notebook passed around to students who wrote various comments about the faculty. This was a way for the underclassmen to see who was liberal, who was strict, and who said what comments to students. For example, if a teacher had an aversion to gum chewing, there might be a grammatically correct sentence that only read: "You have gum!" Perhaps there would be a comment on homework that would read, "Teacher always collects homework at end of class so you can correct it first." If a teacher was over forty years old, someone would state: "She is ancient." On the other hand, if a teacher was liberal and well liked there would be comments that read, "Cool and groovy!" We had our own version of ratemyprofessor.com before the computer age. I read the slam books every chance I could get; the humorous comments brought me great enjoyment.

Along with slam books came the contraband "mature reading books" to help junior high school students learn how to deal with the opposite sex. One of these books circulated during my freshman year was *The Happy Hooker* by Xavier Hollander. Rather than leave the book in my locker until study hall, I would carry it with me, but buried in the bundle of my many textbooks. One day while sitting at the lab table in Life Science class directly in front of the teacher's desk my science teacher spoke to me in a quiet voice, "Isn't that some mature reading material you have there?" Knowing exactly what she was referring to but attempting to save my skin I replied, "I'm reading up on the presidential candidates for the upcoming election." Of course, she had been teaching for far too long to believe that response. "I'm referring to the paperback book you're reading that is about the Happy Hooker!" Things were now out in the open and I expected to be sent to the principal's office again. Instead, still in a quiet voice she went on, "Is it any good?" I was never sent to the principal's office but instead engaged in a brief conversation with my now-favorite science teacher about a high priced call girl who decided to write about her escapades and make even more money.

There was plenty of dating and romancing going on in my junior high school years; however, I stayed away from it because I wasn't comfortable with any of it, I didn't want a baby under any circumstances, thus experimented only with necking with older boys who were outside of the school group. The gossip and stories were a constant theme in a one-horse town and I wanted no part of it. None of it appealed to me. I knew nothing about flirting and had a short attention span for the boys with macho attitudes.

My grades were not the only thing slipping in junior high, my behavior followed suit as well. I was associating with less than stellar students and their behavior was less than stellar as well. I never fully forgot the fact that life as I knew it would end in two to five years so thinking ahead was not possible for me, combined with the low self esteem of being different. I knew from a young age to keep my thoughts to myself to avoid punishment. I knew that everything I knew about myself was considered to be wrong and perverted, not to mention forbidden in my parent's home. I knew I was trapped there and had to survive any way I could.

I was always in trouble for cutting classes, being late to class, or a poor attitude combined with decreasing grades. This was the only the beginning. As the years went on, I would be suspended from school for larger offenses. One infraction I accomplished by pure accident, although no one believed me, which was no surprise given my track record. I was on my way to study hall one late morning and was dragging the tips of my fingers along the wall. Lunch periods had just begun and I was scheduled to go to lunch the next class period. As my fingers were trailing leisurely along the wall, I accidently tripped the fire alarm. I was shocked that such a delicate touch would cause it to go off, but off it went. I watched in horror as the entire school building emptied to the outdoor campus. My gangs of peers were laughing but I knew I had committed a major offense; fire drills were never practiced during lunch periods. There was nothing left to do but turn myself in and accept the consequences. My mother was called in for a conference with my principal, who was actually in a pleasant mood that day. Before he suspended me for three days he announced that I had provided a record time for the books; the building had never evacuated so quickly. Of course I went home to a good beating from my mother, who was embarrassed and humiliated with my behavior.

Just like many students with low self esteem, I started drinking and smoking during my junior high years. Alcohol was easy to obtain within my peer group; after all, many of our parents drank including my father and would not necessarily keep track of reserves. Smoking was something that the majority of the population engaged in. Most of my favorite teachers smoked and although they knew the student body smoked, there was never a crusade to end it. Nor were there any educational programs that taught us about the ill effects of drugs in general. However, if we were caught with cigarettes on our person or caught in the act of smoking itself, that was a situation that demanded punishment.

During my lunch period one late spring morning, my assistant principal caught me with a transistor radio: a contraband item. Along with the radio I had a pack of cigarettes displayed in my front breast pocket. As he approached my table, he could see both items in my shirt breast pocket and demanded both. I was escorted to the main office and given a session with my principal. He was looking out for my best interests when he attempted to counsel me. He reminded me of my religious background and asked me why my behavior was not better since I knew the difference between right and wrong. I could only hang my head; how could I explain to him that everything was coming to an end within the next two years? Instead I apologized for breaking the rules and stated that I would try to improve. I knew that I was in for a horrible beating from my mother, and to make matters worse, I was required to take home a written letter stating that I was caught smoking on school property. I was unable to face the punishment that would be inevitable from my enraged mother. I thought perhaps the best solution to the problem would be to jump off the bridge one block away from my school building. This would end everything: my unavoidable punishment, my low self esteem, my poor health, and most importantly, waiting for Armageddon to arrive. As the afternoon announcements were made that day, I listened to the list of assemblies that were listed on the school calendar, thinking I would not be there to attend any of them. There was calmness in feeling that way. I felt under so much pressure and unable to function in the way that events were progressing.

I walked to the bridge and started to climb on top of the railing as I looked down to the shallow river below. Then, the thought occurred to me, what if I was I to survive? My body would be broken and in worse shape than it already was, and perhaps taking my chances in an upcoming concentration camp for political prisoners might be a better option. I turned around and walked the two blocks home knowing that I was in for a severe punishment. Punishments from my mother would include a good beating along with long-term consequences that would continue for weeks during those awful years. My teachers were aware that things were less than normal on the home-front but during the early seventies there was not the awareness or involvement from professional staff on the front lines.

A part of my punishment would include forced feminization: I was not allowed to wear slacks to school anymore, I was to help with the cooking required for dinner every night, and on Saturday afternoons I would take sewing lessons from a sister in the congregation. I would be grounded, or in other words, confined to the public areas of the house with no phone calls or outside contact with anyone. My music would be taken away and my bedroom was searched on a regular basis for any contraband material. Of course, when I left for school I would roll my skirts up at the waist; miniskirts were all the rage then. Punishments were brutal; however, I was never kept from being in school for punishment and that is what saved me.

During my freshman year the Vietnam War came to an end and we started to finally withdraw troops from Southeast Asia. When this happened we went into our advanced placement history class and wrote our comments of relief and joy all over the blackboard, however elementary and trivial they must have been at the time.

My health continued to be a problem with more time at home sick and away from school. I had started to see an ear, nose and throat specialist because my ears were always infected multiple times throughout the year. He told my parents that there was fluid in my ears that needed to be drained immediately and if not, it would be impossible to drain in the future and I would suffer permanent hearing loss. I wondered if this was what had happened to my paternal grandfather as he had been deaf most of his life. My parents had me admitted to the hospital for surgery to have things corrected. This was before healthcare was in shambles, and outpatient procedures were in the way distant future. I was admitted the night before, had surgery the next morning and then stayed in the hospital for an additional day before being released. When I came out of the recovery department and back to my room, I was shocked at how loud every sound had become. More than that, I was grateful to have my hearing back.

Despite the fact that Armageddon was just around the corner, life went on. My parents decided to remodel the third floor of their home, giving me my own bedroom with a guest bedroom on the other side of the third floor. This all seemed to fit into the extreme spectrum that ruled my life: one minute

I was not to be trusted with my bedroom searched for contraband, and the next minute I was given my own space with privacy on a different floor of the house.

My father hired an old-school Italian carpenter who had great skills, and to save money, my sister and I were in charge of the cleanup required after he departed for the day. I was also allowed to pick out my own carpeting and furniture. My father was able to purchase my bedroom furniture from his job at a discount. I chose a masculine and stark style of furniture that would be appropriate for a teenage boy's bedroom. Yet, I was permitted to indulge in such a masculine choice. My carpet was a shag multicolored red and orange, all the rage in the mid 1970's.

Life would continue on with the death of both of my mother's parents within one month of each other, despite the fact they had been apart for over thirty years. My grandmother died of ovarian cancer in my parents' home; her last three months of life were hard on my mother as the cancer slowly robbed her of life. She required twenty-four-hour care; because my mother had the most resources, it was decided that she would have the final watch. In her final months of life, my grandmother would hallucinate due to her high fevers, which led her to think she was back on the farm. She would call me up to her room; tell me that there had been an accident in front of the house and to summon police. I would assist in her custodial care helping to deliver meals to her bed; always soft foods because she had lost her teeth decades earlier. She was never able to escape the poverty that strangled her life beginning as a young adult. There were no women's rights when she came of age, no birth control, and very few ways for a woman to be independent in a man's world. Thus, there were too many children with too few resources to ever crawl out of the endless hole that poverty creates.

As the end drew closer more and more family members and members of the congregation would stop over to the house to help provide respite to my mother in any way possible. As a teenager, I was painfully aware of the devastating effects that both cancer and the chemo treatments had on my grandmother. I watched her go from someone who was full of life to a skeletal figure weighing not more than one hundred pounds. The constant pain had etched permanent lines on her forehead with her voice and laughter all but gone. She had huge bedsores from being bedridden because this was long before advanced mattresses that would help distribute body weight and better blood flow. Although my grandmother was only in her early sixties she looked as though she were in her eighties. This was a combination of lifelong poverty, childbirth nine times over, combined with a deadly disease. My grandmother was very intelligent; however, she was plagued with poor health through all of her life. She would read a book to escape from the world; her interests spanned from history, anthropology, criminology, the classics, even cheap paperback drugstore novels. As an adult I began to understand that my grandmother was brilliant as I read her endless library that had been saved. I realized as well that brilliance is only part of the equation: to be successful there must be intelligence combined with good health along with a time in history that would allow women's rights.

Within that same year, tragedy would strike again. My mother's younger brother would be in a car accident, swerving left of center and killing his girlfriend who was riding in the passenger seat. He would be charged with vehicular homicide. Also, my mother's younger sister who had battled depression for her entire life would commit suicide. She was missing and was found three days later floating in a river after jumping from a bridge. She would leave behind a husband and three children, the youngest three years old. The funerals seemed to never end that year, along with the grief that enveloped my mother's family. As a teenager I was not permitted to ask questions or to listen to the adult conversations, yet there was much adult conversation. A huge family, each one dealing with their grief in their own way: some arguing about what should have maybe been done, some grief about not understanding why the events had happened the way they had with young children being left with only one less-than-functional parent, and of course the question of what to do next.

Throughout elementary school my sister and I had been close and would play together; I would always look out for her at school since I was the oldest and was told that I was to be more mature and the leader. However, when I started junior high school things changed; I was becoming "too cool" to spend time with her, especially since I was spending as much time as possible with my gang of peers who became my surrogate family. Not only was I excluded from the adults' conversation, I now did not talk to my younger sister anymore.

Once we had drifted apart, it would remain that way for decades, especially when I was able to hide in my own bedroom. We were two children sharing a home but each of us dealing with our own lives silently. As we matured we would take separate paths into adulthood.

NINE

By the time I was in high school everything had changed. I was still involved in advanced history and English classes but was also able to take classes that I excelled in such as speech and drama. My friends that I had in junior high school had gone their separate ways. After all, this was high school and we were all grown up because things were more serious and important. I still had excellent teachers and a group of friends who supported me, but there wasn't the intense intimacy that there had been in junior high school. All of a sudden everything became more important: classes, sports and extra-curricular activities. Dating and social status became more important as did wardrobe and the current fashion with the concern of who wore what. I continued to drink and drive around in sports cars with older boys who were not from my high school. I would do this in the morning before school would start, a short ride to start the day, just enough for me to feel as though I had rebelled and broken the rules. I would announce to my mother that an early arrival to school was needed for an additional informal study hall with my classmates. I survived with my status of outsider, not part of any crowd since scriptural doctrine still forbid any more contact with the world than was necessary in public education. I wanted to be involved more in the student life that was offered; after all, it was a large and traditional part of the high school experience. However, each student body has a group of general students who aren't involved in all that's offered, so I wasn't the only one and that was comforting.

I started thinking about getting a job and began babysitting every weekend that I could get hired. I was so grateful to be earning money because money meant independence; I had no desire to go out with boys on a Saturday night and preferred to be employed instead.

During my sophomore year my health would begin to decline further exposing genetic defects that had to be dealt with. On a Friday afternoon in the autumn, I attended a football pep rally in the gymnasium with all the high school in attendance, complete with cheering, and school spirit abundant in the air. My lower back started to hurt and as the afternoon wore on became the worst pain I had felt in my short life. Upon getting home from school I went straight to bed. My mother noticed my disappearance and investigated why I gone to my bedroom so quickly. She asked the usual questions a parent would ask: was it something I had eaten, did I perhaps pull a muscle, had I been in a fight with anyone? As I responded "no!" to every question, there was little to do but monitor the situation. As the night wore on, the pain got worse and urinating became a painful and bloody ordeal. I requested to go to the emergency room; I knew that between the pain and blood in my urine I was sick.

As I stumbled down the stairs and into my mother's car at almost midnight, my father arrived drunk. That started an argument between my parents as my mother reminded my father that he should be the one transporting me to the hospital. My father reminded my mother that he was out working late to pay for the medical bills that I was incurring. I was looking forward to receiving medical attention because I was so sick yet had to listen to the both of them arguing like children. After at last getting to the emergency room, a urine specimen was collected. At that time the procedure involved urinating into a clear glass specimen bottle. My urine was black with blood and I knew that something was very wrong when I glanced over and saw the specimen bottle. I was admitted immediately and my pediatrician, who had been called in, came and sat on the edge of my bed. In a fatherly tone, he explained to me that I was very sick and despite the fact that I was still a minor he was turning me over to a doctor who would be able to help me. I was in the hospital for three days and once again missing school for a week. I was given a course of antibiotics for my diagnosed bladder infection. This would be the beginning of ongoing infections that would last until I was twenty-two years old and paying for my own medical care.

The last two years of high school would be in vocational school; a decision I made and would regret for years. I would start my junior year of high school in September of 1974, with Armageddon slated for a mere four months away. I wanted something different and even though I had good friends, the friendships weren't strong enough for me to stay at my high school. I would be in a new school with new classmates instead of the group I had advanced with since kindergarten. My new classmates would come from all around the county to a building that embraced the open classroom concept. There were no walls, only pods with movable cabinets that served as storage and walls. Very opposite from the traditional high school that I attended for a year. Vocational schools and trade schools are an important component in our educational system; however, I should have stayed at my high school since I was there for all of the wrong reasons. I was numb to everything around me; I didn't care about school, and lacked any sort of self-awareness except fear.

I was still thinking there was some truth in the 1975 deadline; a war would start, I would be forced underground, society would become like Germany in World War II. My father had retired at this point; he had taken all of his retirement out in preparation for the unknown. Everyone in the congregation was gearing up in their own personal way with fear and paranoia. I had thoughts of never graduating from high school come June of 1976; that was past the deadline of the battle between God and Satan. Why stay in high school? Why not try something totally different? Especially when the school year may only last four months; with my life on autopilot I just put one foot in front of the other one and went through life numb and full of fear. At this point my mother seemed to give up on punishing me, perhaps thinking I would be judged within the next year in all ways that were important.

My teachers at the vocational school were as nontraditional as my building with the males sporting long hair and open collar shirts, not the traditional suit and short hair that had been present at my high school. The cafeteria had students serving us lunch on plates instead of institutional trays. Our yearbook was totally produced by students; the photography and art students contributed their talents, and the books were printed at our school by students who studied printing as a trade. Some of my classmates from my high school were also there with me and that was comforting.

My school friends were part of one gang; in addition, I had a work gang that provided me with support from yet another set of peers. When I turned sixteen, I went to the Social Security Office and got my social security card to begin working and paying taxes. Some of my friends were seeking employment at fast food establishments and I thought this would be as good a place as any to work. Because I was a baby boomer and there were five people for every one job opening, I went back three different times before I was actually hired. Once again, I made friends along with a new set of skills. We worked well together, all of us young, idealistic and naïve. We never thought about the fact that we were working for a billion dollar company who was exploiting us with minimum wage pay: one dollar and ninety cents an hour. Considering I had been babysitting for fifty cents an hour, it was a pay raise and more freedom for me.

Before I got the job my manager said to my older neighbor who also was employed there, "He is going to have to cut that long hair before he is allowed to work here." My neighbor explained that since I was female that chore wouldn't be necessary. In spite of the initial misunderstanding, the people I worked with once again became my support system and I loved the job because of that. We all learned teamwork, networking, dealing with the public, and it was one of the best jobs I've ever had. In addition to that, I developed friendships from that job that I still maintain at midlife. Most of us were teenagers and at times acted our age, playing practical jokes on one another. We would often go out together after our shift was over to drink and smoke. I was able to buy alcohol underage because I looked so much older. Those were delightful times for me; my coworkers accepted me for who I was without criticism. Management protected me by keeping me in the back and working on the grill, a job reserved for the males with the females working the counter and taking the food orders.

Sexual discrimination laws didn't exist in 1975 and the male upper management who only stopped in occasionally knew that. There was an older male manager who would stop in and make his rounds with all of the girls, standing too close, violating personal space, rubbing up against them or brushing up against their breasts. He was crass in his language and during staff meetings would announce that he had better see the girls moving their asses faster when there were customers waiting at the counter. When he attempted to fondle my best friend Cheryl, she protested; he declared there would be consequences for her insubordination. She announced that she didn't care about any consequences; he needed to keep his hands to himself. Although I would dread his arrival to our store, I never protested since I knew at that young age that he had all the power.

My job also allowed me more independence than I had ever had. I would tell my mother I was working until eleven at night, but then get off at eight and spend the evening drinking with my coworkers. When alcohol is involved poor judgment can easily follow; I always had beer in the back of my trunk with my own money to buy as much as I could afford. My mother never monitored my paychecks to see how many hours I actually worked so I had some free time built in for friendships. One warm spring evening I had a carload of teenage boys from work in my car and we were all enjoying a few beers and cruising around the town. During that time cars were well built and gasoline was cheap. A ride around town with alcohol was one of the most exciting things we could do. Conversation and gossip flowed with topics ranging from the latest rock music to the latest news from the workplace. I was driving a 1970 Buick LaSabre: a Detroit product with real steel that included an interior that held six people comfortably. I was far underneath the legal limit for drunk driving but was feeling happy and free. We were in a rural area where we would frequently escape to the quiet and darkness of no city lights. I drove into a Dairy Queen that had a long line due to being the only place where young people could gather. In the line, there were two soldiers who looked quite handsome, complete with pride and attitude.

When they noticed me, the snickering and pointing started, along with their curiosity as to what exactly had just gotten out of that Buick. Was it male or female? I was flanked by my best friend Dale and another coworker, both of them of slight build, thin and looking gay in a town full of boys who attempted to be macho. I could see the soldiers starting to bristle and I knew the hateful verbiage would be next. When the situation involved fight or flight, I was one to take flight since I didn't know how to fight. We all scrambled back to my car but before we pulled out of the parking lot Kevin rolled down his window and announced, "It's a girl, so stop your staring, you jerks!" That was all it took and the soldiers were in their car chasing us down a dark two lane country road. I was worried that they would try to rear-end me so when they got too close, I went into the other lane, each of us pushing ninety miles per hour. I finally gave up after going miles over the speed limit and into the oncoming lane of traffic on a dark country road. I had started my teenage adolescent angst that would continue for the next six years: stupid and deadly behavior simply because for the first time in my life I could participate in such destruction.

I was trying hard to be female during those years and decided to partake in the high school rite of passage of my junior prom. I took the liberty of asking a coworker if he would attend with me. He wasn't dating anyone steady at the time and perhaps was relieved that I had extended the invitation: those thoughts and conversations about feelings were not common in 1975. I felt daring, thinking I should get one prom under my belt before Armageddon struck, with my mother remarkably allowing me to attend. I didn't ask why she seemed to have a change of heart; by this time I knew to stay out of the way of her wrath by being absent as much as possible from home. Working was permitted and I used that to my full advantage. My prom night was held at my local high school and the band that played that night included a drummer who attended Catholic school and also worked with both my date and me. The song, "Rebel Rebel" by David Bowie was popular then and Bowie was one of my heroes. My mother would scream at me that between David Bowie and the shock-rock group Kiss, I only had men on my bedroom wall that wore makeup which was disgusting. I, on the other hand, was eternally grateful that these artists were popular during my youth because they told me that there was someone like me in the world.

As my date and I entered the building, David the drummer in the band looked up to view our arrival just as the song, "Rebel Rebel" was starting. He smiled and shouted into the microphone that the song was being dedicated to me and I couldn't have felt more honored: lyrics speaking of a mother who is in a whirl because she can't tell if her child is a boy or a girl. Despite my trying to be female, at very best I was only androgynous. Usually seen as male and at second glance maybe androgynous female but hardly ever at first glance seen as born a female. No matter what clothes I wore–rabbit fur coat, lacy blouse, girls' leather boots–none of the exterior wardrobe seemed to matter. People seemed to have various theories as to why this was: I was too tall, my voice was too deep, my glasses frames too masculine. I weighed a mere one hundred and fifty pounds on an almost six foot frame, and was far from healthy, constantly sick with some sort of internal infection: my ears, my bladder, my sinuses. With very small breasts, I even tried a slightly padded bra and read the women's magazines to follow the latest style and mold me into the kind of women I was supposed to be when I grew up, even though I felt connected to none of it. I cut my long hair, went to a hairdresser to have curls and waves to only my shoulders. I plucked my bushy eyebrows even though Ali McGraw had changed that female landscape of facial hair in *Love Story*. I would cut out pictures of her face from the magazines and study them. She had refused to pluck her eyebrows into the thin feathered line and I loved her rebelling against that feminine trend. I was trying so hard to mold myself into what society wanted me to become yet knowing I was different but also knowing that I needed to survive even if Armageddon was just around the corner.

Although most of my friends were guys, my feelings toward females were strong and I would have secret crushes on various girls although I was careful to keep them well hidden. However, one night in 1974 while at the Kingdom Hall I met an authentic "California girl" whom I couldn't get out of my mind. She was visiting friends in my congregation and lived in a suburb just outside of San Francisco. I was smitten with her mature ways; she was a few years older and had already dropped out of high school since Armageddon was soon to arrive and it was a waste of her time. She would speak of how she would walk down her high school halls thinking of how all of her classmates would just be gone in a year. She gave me a picture and on the back advised me to continue serving Jehovah and then signed it, "See you on the other side, Kate." When she returned to California I wrote and called, and she would be in my life for the next thirteen years.

This was a major turning point in my life and one that I faced entirely alone. I was never close to either of my parents, and so was left to figure out how to approach a life I had never expected to live. The year of 1975 which seemed to be one of the longest in my life eventually came to an end with me also turning eighteen at the very end of the year and realizing it had all been a scam. There was no Armageddon of course; I was in my senior year of high school due to graduate within the next six months, with no idea what I was going to do with the rest of my life, a life that I had never expected but would now take place. I had no future plans with the world still being intact; now I would need to become a part of society. I still attended vocational school and was only attending school half the day with working day shift in fast food for the remainder of the day. I had wasted my last two years of high school: no advance college preparatory classes, no job skills, and not even any thought that I would end up still alive to start my life as an adult.

I did attend my senior prom with another coworker whom I once again asked to accompany me. Tragedy would end our friendship: within the next few months he would die in a boating accident. The funeral was heartbreaking with all of us from work at his burial place with his coworkers carrying his coffin to his grave site. His devastated family stood beside us along with his many friends and I found myself wondering how I could be alive and lose him. We don't know what life has in store for us, and I had no idea this was only the beginning of the losses that I would face in my adult life.

This was the 1970's, and I attended public school before school shootings and violence. I will always be grateful but am saddened that the world has so drastically changed for the next generation who followed me. Of course we experienced all the emotions of teenagers; however, the thought of killing someone never entered our minds.

My father now retired with no job, sat in the backyard, drank his alcohol and stared off into nowhere. He was a broken man although there was never any conversation that we were now into the next calendar year and the world was still here. He would become more and more absent from home until eventually moving out altogether. He would eventually go back to work, although when he cashed in his retirement he lost a huge amount of money because it was around the time that Nixon had resigned and the stock market was down. He was never the same after 1975 and became bitter, more enraged and would eventually leave the religion altogether when his alcoholism consumed more and more of his life and money. With his alcoholism out of control, he would get drunk and tell my sister and me that he had never wanted children and it was my mother's idea. Relief would come when he would leave the house for days and go live with his other family.

I had been writing Kate regularly this entire time, now in a panic that I had to decide what I was going to do for the rest of my life. My mother had taught me excellent money skills; I always saved money at every turn. In the summer of 1976, after my high school graduation, I flew to California to see Kate, her roommate sister, and of course San Francisco. This was the first time I was ever away from my home and my parents but because Kate attended the Kingdom Hall, I had my mother's approval. Flying in 1976 involved checking your bags, buying a nonstop flight for two hundred dollars and arriving at the airport fifteen minutes before the plane departed down the runway. Both of my parents were to transport me to the airport and my father showed up after a night of drinking with bloodshot eyes and clothes that looked as though he had slept in them. Of course another parental argument would ensue and I would be forced to listen since I was trapped in the car with both of them for hours.

Kate was working in a manual labor job: cleaning apartments in the complex where she lived since she had never completed high school or invested in any sort of job training. Just as with all other Jehovah's Witnesses, the subject of Armageddon being a lie was never discussed. Instead there were hushed tones of the date being wrong but of course the event was still going to happen. I knew to avoid the subject with both her and her sister as they still both believed all that the Watchtower Bible and Tract Society told them. I arrived with gifts and cash for my share of the rent. Because I was a guest in their apartment, I attended meetings at the Kingdom Hall. I never spoke to or met anyone else who was not involved in the religion and I wanted to get to San Francisco's gay district so I decided to go alone.

I was only eighteen and had never been on my own before and the adrenaline combined with the energy was hard for me to contain. I had never taken public transportation much less handled a large city like the city by the bay. I took buses to the Bay Area Rapid Transit, boarded the BART and exited at Market Street in the city. I had no map, no agenda and no plan. I walked for miles, block after block, enjoying the sites. While at a traffic light that had just barely gone from yellow to red, I ran as fast as I could and made it across before the light changed. A deep voice announced from a Cadillac so close I was able to touch it, "I should have killed you and next time I will." I had ended up somehow in the Tenderloin district of the city, unaware in my excitement that block after block had been declining into poverty complete with prostitutes on every corner. I walked up to a sex shop arranged with a heart shaped window and two women in tight blouses and cleavage, and boldly asked directions to the gay district. Directions were given and I was then on my way to Polk Street feeling as though the world was mine. While at a record store I struck up a conversation with a man who was also alone. As one thing led to another I found myself stupidly going back to his apartment, a decision that could have been fatal. We talked for a while and then I realized the next step was going to be sex and I bolted for the door, running down four flights of stairs out into the street to the nearest bus station. The last bus for the night back to the BART station was ready to pull away but I made it. Wanting to cram as much as I could into my time there and knowing Kate was only associating with Jehovah's

Witnesses, I realized that if I wanted to speak to a true gay person I would need to seek them on my own.

Music and any kind of performance art has always been a love of mine so when I discovered that The Manhattan Transfer was appearing in San Francisco, I went to the vintage stores on Polk Street and bought Kate and I vintage dresses for the occasion. We were like two school girls dressing up; I was excited to appear in a costume dress for the fun and pictures. We set out into the city for a wonderful concert and dinner at a five start restaurant. As we were walking to the restaurant, a woman richly dressed in a fur wrap, beautiful dress and perfect makeup approached us with her husband warning us to get off the streets because we were not in a safe area. She was giving motherly advice to two girls who were young and excited, unaware of the high crime in the city.

Visiting the gay district of San Francisco would go on until 1988; I would visit Kate and the city alone whenever I was able to obtain enough cash to pay for the trip. Each time I was there I would head to the gay district to chat with store clerks and servers. I was unable to maintain any lasting connections. Kate and I would drift farther and farther apart over the years as our lives took us in different directions. She became a divorced mother of two while I preferred to live in a city that was as supportive of my way of life as possible; eventually we lost contact.

TEN

In 1976 I would leave fast food when I returned and head into the factories for full time employment and the health benefits that I desperately needed since once I turned eighteen medical insurance was my concern and no longer my parents. I still didn't know what to do with my life and was struggling with horrible bouts of depression. I felt alone, confused and afraid, with many of my peers heading off to college. I wanted to join them but didn't know what I would major in and then there was my health. I was still getting bladder infections, and seeing a urologist who would give me antibiotics to clear them up. There were still numerous infections in my ears, throat, and sinuses. I was absent from work more than employers would permit and within the next three years would obtain work at three different factories and be terminated from two of them because of missing more than the allowable sick time.

Working in fiberglass and titanium was brutal physical work and most times monotonous, performing the same function of moving a fiberglass part through a sander, press drill or grinder. I would daydream by the hour about leaving to live in a major city where I belonged instead of the small rural town that I was living in. The highest paying factories had seen their glory days and were already shut down. The remaining jobs were a dollar above minimum wage with no union protection and rarely included proper safety equipment. I took my turn in getting injured with a drill press slamming into my left wrist, and skin disappearing down to the bone. They called my emergency contact for a trip to the hospital and my father showed up in a fit of rage that I had not been more careful. After I was bandaged up and dismissed to go home I passed out on the floor of the hospital lobby. The last thing I remember seeing is people running in what seemed to be slow motion. This was the beginning of me having a seizure disorder due to having such poor kidneys.

In the factories every year I would see someone lose fingers and go out in an ambulance. The people who worked at industrial jobs were poor and kept to themselves, although at one of the factories, a woman that I worked night shift with went home that morning, took a twelve gauge shotgun and killed her husband on the way up from the basement stairs. I put the article that was the front page headlines from the local paper into my scrapbook along with my first plane ticket to San Francisco and the picture of Christine Jorgensen, who was one of the first persons to become widely known in the United States for having sexual reassignment surgery. During this time in history, Jorgensen was one of the few who had gone public with sexual reassignment surgery. I now knew there were others out there like me which was a tremendous comfort in dealing with the loneliness that I felt.

Because I had health insurance I began to see a therapist to attempt to put my life into the present and prepare for a future that I never thought would arrive. I would always feel behind in the world, I would be late in beginning all of my transitions that were required in adulthood. In addition, I was beginning an adult life in a world that I knew nothing about. I never thought I would live this long. Here I was an adult needing to navigate and function in society; so in those early years my counseling was more educational than anything. I had been raised such an isolationist I had little knowledge of much of anything. Even so, beginning therapy at the age of eighteen was one of the best things I ever accomplished and I would go back to it whenever I needed to for the next two decades.

Many parts of my life were not where they needed to be and I was attempting to sort through all of the intense emotions that came with that. I needed to go to college, to support myself, get to a better city that accepted people who were like me. I was unable to control my anger, depressions, and very poor physical health that constantly made me exhausted. I had never talked to anyone who was gay or transgender, I had only read about them in a few books. I lived in a void of any information with no internet, no social media, and very little news coverage of anything that involved gay or transgender people except to report the negative. For example, my mother would talk of a sting operation that focused on the Greyhound bus station men's bathroom that involved local men getting arrested for "homosexual activity." Of course, everyone involved in the arrest had their names printed in the local paper and lost their jobs as a result of the shameful publicity.

Any feelings that I had, I kept them to myself and as soon as I was eighteen I started therapy. Although therapy was helpful, it had been only three years earlier, in 1973, that the American Psychiatric Association had taken homosexuality off their books as a mental illness. So although the therapists weren't trying to change my sexual orientation, they weren't trained that well in how to deal with someone who was gay, lesbian, bisexual or transgender. Mental health and medicine were barely beyond the infancy stages in my small town. There were no MRI machines that could capture the inside of a human body within minutes, there were only X-Ray machines. Blood work would take weeks to be checked for any desired answers. A trip to the hospital would take a week and a test a day would be performed with the results taking days instead of hours. Small towns aren't known for their teaching hospitals and good medical care. I knew to get medical attention when I would get an ear infection and blood in my urine. The result would always be antibiotics to clear the infection and nothing more, even with a specialist in the field.

I would work in the factories from 1976 until 1979 when I would begin college and start the new decade of the 1980's. While working in the factories I met a coworker named Lyn who was older but friendly enough and we struck up a friendship. She and I would spend time drinking and sometimes we would go out to the local bars together. During one of these nights night I was able to meet someone who was gay, and before long he and I would be going to the gay clubs that were located in a major city hours away. Donna Summer was playing on the turntable and the clubs were packed with men dancing the night away. This was just before AIDS hit and the world was ours to dance into the night. I also for the first time saw "drag queens" in action and I immediately felt a kinship with them. They too had been born in a gender that they decided to rebel against and wear women's clothes and perform on stage.

From the moment that I walked into my first gay club I knew that my life would get better because there were people like me and for the first time in my life I fit in; I felt that I could survive in the world because I had support. I would spend those years drinking far too much, going to the gay clubs and living with Lyn. By this time my father had left my childhood home and my mother had gone into the workforce making minimum wage in an attempt to be able to keep the house. My father had taken his retirement savings to support his other family and there was no money. My mother fought for the house because that was all that was left of a marriage over long ago. My sister and I would take care of the grocery shopping, yard, and housecleaning while she worked long hours at a retail job. We became three strangers never talking, never discussing the Armageddon that never happened or how things had gone so horribly wrong. We were all in survival mode, each of us focusing on the next chapter of our respective lives. My sister and I were both planning our lives and my mother was trying to save her house.

My health continued to spiral downward and I was passing out more and more from seizures. I attempted to work night shift and that is when my health really spiraled downward, with a trip to the hospital and a new doctor. I was diagnosed with a seizure disorder and put on medication to control the seizures which allowed me a better life and my attendance improved at the factory. My coworkers were never that friendly toward me, many of them older women who seemed to be afraid of me. Once while at the vending machines in the break room, fishing for change in my pocket, I apparently came too close to a co-worker's purse located in a neighboring chair. She bolted toward me and grabbed her purse and I responded with a look of shock. I then realized how they perceived me as someone who was different and thus deviant.

By January of 1979, I enrolled in college at a regional branch campus. I would take Freshman English and the three credit hours would cost me thirty-three dollars. Finally starting college was one of the best things I could have done with my life. Previously, I had done nothing but drink too much and work in a job that I was overqualified for and live a stagnant life. Even though I was now an adult, I still was flirting with being female and even attempted to date men. Of the two men that I attempted to date, one was fairly fun; the other was a disaster that ended with an attempted date rape. That incident ended any attempt to bond with straight men and instead I focused on going to class, studying and working full time in the factories. By the spring of 1979, I was enrolled full time in college and went to work part time doing any sort of employment that I could find. I worked retail, cleaned houses, all at minimum wage, but I was ecstatic that my life was finally going in a positive direction. I had wonderful professors, small classes and met people who were not from my small town, but from other cities. They were beginning their careers in professional jobs, changing careers, or perhaps taking a break before heading into a new career. All of this helped me go into a world that had not been a part of my life growing up. I was naïve, inexperienced in all things worldly; everyone I met contributed something to my personal growth. I set out to mend the damage that I had done in high school and enrolled in a liberal arts curriculum, taking subjects in history and English that I should have taken in high school.

As we started the 1980s with all that history would bring us, I was in the hospital three times and was finally diagnosed with a double ureter on my right kidney that was infected and needed to be removed. I was sent to a larger, better equipped hospital in a city hours away with a surgeon who specialized in urology. Because it was major surgery and a serious operation, both of my parents were required to be at the consultation. Within minutes upon the doctor's exit my parents were in a huge argument, my father demanding to know why the problem hadn't been discovered years ago especially with all the money he spent on medical bills. My mother retorted with the reminder that the money went to his other family, with me finally demanding that both of them leave my hospital room to finish the argument elsewhere.

I was horribly anemic at this point and weighed only one hundred thirty five pounds on a nearly six foot frame. I had been plagued with chronic bladder infections that would not stop for the last four years and had been to three different doctors trying to remedy the problem. Finally finding the problem was a relief but I was exhausted from being sick and just wanted to get the problem resolved. The doctor was concerned that with my low blood count, there may be a possibility for a necessary blood transfusion. Although I didn't believe most of what the Watchtower Bible and Tract Society now taught, I didn't want a blood transfusion. So I signed a release of liability and the doctor promised that if the surgery required a transfusion, he would stop, sew me up, build my blood up with more B-12 shots and go in for more surgery six months later. Because I was in such bad shape, the B-12 shots had been ongoing for a week right up until they wheeled me down to surgery. A young nursing assistant shaved my groin the night before surgery. Taking a long shower afterwards, I looked at my unscarred body knowing it would never look the same. I was twenty-two, still fighting horrible depressions, still feeling so far behind my peers in comparison to the accomplishments in their lives. Now I was in for another roadblock. I knew the recovery time would be long, preventing me from attending college. I thought about the risk of surgery and all that was involved and didn't care if something went wrong and I did not survive the operation. I knew that my mother was worried because my sister had accompanied my mother after she had a private consultation with the doctor, and after slamming the obligatory gift of boxed candy on my nightstand my sister leaned over and whispered, "It's really bad!"

The day of surgery before I was even given pre-surgery drugs, a phlebotomist was in at 5:00 AM taking more blood from me and thanking me for my patience when he was unable to find a vein. I was so tired of being poked and probed with needles, exploratory bladder surgery three times over, urinating on a table while they X-Rayed me in an attempt to see if the problem was bladder or kidney, what was one more painful stick? I was being prepped to go under the knife, my body forever altered and I had my doubts that it was finally going to get better. My glasses were removed and the world became distant, blurry, disoriented. I could see the outline of the lights overhead, square and bright, blaring down on me as they took me to the operating room. I could hear the wheels on the gurney grinding the linoleum floor until it all stopped and I was placed on the table. Drugs were administered, the process all too familiar for me but I wasn't prepared for the cold that made me start to shiver and not stop. Someone placed a blanket over me and someone else checked my chart. Out of the din I could hear a female voice, no doubt a nurse, say, "Oh my god, we've got the wrong one." Mistakes happen every day in the medical profession and I found myself wondering what operation I almost got that I wasn't scheduled for that day. I was relocated to another room, another table, and then came another needle with the cold liquid flowing into my right arm.

I woke up and saw my friend Lyn crying on a telephone that was on my nightstand next to a dozen red roses. For a second I didn't know where I was until the pain started. I could hear Linda telling someone on the phone that it was horrible, there were tubes full of blood everywhere around me. I was numb from my breasts down to below my groin, yet the searing pain came from deep inside: muscular rather than skeletal. The ordeal had taken six hours and that was the easy portion of the journey as I had slept through it all. Recovering now began: it was at that time I realized how sick I had really been. In fact, it was as though I had gone from the brink of death back to life. I was in the hospital for two weeks; this was before insurance companies dictated the amount of time allowed post-op. The only people making the decisions were my doctors. My diet consisted of liquids for over a week, not that I had much of an appetite. I was extremely weak and was unable to get my legs up on the bed without help after they had been lowered to the floor. It took two nurses to hold me up to be able to walk from my bed to the door and back to the bed again. Each day I would continue to walk farther out of the room into the hall and eventually I was able to walk on my own, over a week later.

I finally summoned the courage to look at myself in the mirror days after the knife was stilled and studied the thirteen inches of incisions on two different places on the right side of my torso, one of them almost slicing my groin in half. My whole body was still raw and numb, full of tubes draining the blood from the incisions: a horrible sight to witness in the small bathroom mirror of my hospital room. The morphine helped dull the pain but I could tell when four hours had passed and it was time for another shot. Lying in bed for hours looking at stupid television programs because I was unable to read was unbearable. The boredom, isolation and imprisonment of being in a hospital made each day seem like it would never end. I looked forward to meals even if it was only jello and soup broth. Despite being hours away from my friends, many of them made the drive to visit me. As grateful as I was for their company I went into a deep depression while I was hospitalized. My recovery was going to be a long one, I was unable to work, and I was terrified of what the future held for me. All of my working life I received lowered evaluations and even termination because of my absentee record; now I was unable to walk down the hospital hall much less maintain employment.

After I was discharged my friends helped me to heal piece by piece. I went to the country to convalesce at my best friend Cheryl's house. She was married with two young children but had an extra room and a bathroom on the first floor. I started walking every day, at first only for ten minutes, but I kept at it and eventually was able to slowly increase the time. Prescription high-powered vitamins helped along with my obsession to heal. I would take a year off from college because I was unable to concentrate or read for any length of time. My recovery took that entire year with me working only ten hours a week in retail; progress was extremely slow but somehow I went from pillar to post and kept moving. Feeling in my torso would not return for years and I would protect my right side from harm, real or imagined, for the next decade. My skin felt as though it was frozen from ice cubes and when I touched my torso I was numb. However, the seizures had stopped, and eventually the huge dark circles around my eyes disappeared and the color in my face improved.

I returned to college and declared a major in business to allow me to support myself. Falling in love and depending on someone else wasn't for me; I wanted independence and a good career to achieve that independence. Feeling inadequate was always in the back of my mind, so I wanted to ensure that I would be able to be financially independent and able to live on my own income only. Since gay rights at that time did not exist, I was wise to have this philosophy of independence. In addition, laws that protected heterosexual marriages would never protect me.

One of my psychology classes involved an internship in a small but progressive office that counseled troubled youths. The staff consisted of young and enthusiastic professionals just starting their careers and I enjoyed working under their guidance. I had a set of keys to the office and was alone one Saturday looking for a folder in one of the many file cabinets. While thumbing through the endless manila folders I came across one that had my name in the protruding tab. Curious, I removed it and opened it to find a clandestine report from the secretary of the agency listing all she felt was wrong with my work performance. I had been hired with a male who was a local teacher; yet his name wasn't listed on any manila folder in the filing cabinet. My first encounter in the work world with male privilege had arrived. The secretary was hoping to increase her position within the agency; I was an easy target to narrow in on, in her opinion. After all, I was young, naïve and with a distinct submissive personality. I followed orders without even questioning or complaining, hardly how my male colleague behaved, but he was male and not open to review by a female in a lesser position. A valuable lesson was provided on the working world where I would spend my life. My naiveté and innocence of the world outside of my religious cult had me stinging with shock that someone would perform this action behind my back, never speaking to me first. Copying the report, I would discuss it with my young therapist who seemed shocked as well. I never spoke of it to anyone but took to heart the brutal lesson that in the workplace people are not to be trusted. My supervisor never spoke of it and I received an A for the class and moved on in pursuing my other classes.

In some of my classes, there were opportunities to travel with my classmates at an inexpensive rate, usually utilizing chartered buses. One such opportunity involved visiting New York City and attending three Broadway plays with my theater class. We rode the bus all night and arrived in New York City the following morning. My travel companions were a group of young women who had never been to the city before. Of course, I suggested that we visit Greenwich Village, knowing it was the gay district. As we passed by the sex shops in the village showing leather harnesses and whips in the windows, I attempted with great difficulty to withhold my excitement. My classmates were notably shocked, but I just shrugged it off as a symptom of one of the largest cities in the world. We passed Uncle Charlie's Bar and as I peered into the window and saw not one female, I knew we were in the heart of my world. At one of the many bookstores there was a newspaper, *The Walt Whitman*, which allowed me to smile with great pride. One of my classmates whispered to me, "Do you think this bookstore is gay? Walt Whitman was gay you know." My response was a calming, "Well who knows, maybe." My classmate continued on in a discussion of her own sexuality, detailing how she and her boyfriend were postponing sex until marriage because they both felt it was the right thing to do. "Well that's very honorable, but sex isn't that great anyway, the both of you aren't missing anything," I responded both respectfully and matter-of-factly.

Our visit to New York City was before Times Square had been cleaned up by the mayor and when we dressed to attend sophisticated Broadway shows and walked past various addicts and homeless men, there were whistles and comments from up and down the street. My companions were shocked and fearful with their small town innocence. The city referred to me as sir at every turn with my companions weighing in as to why: it was my glasses, my height, and my deep voice. In reality, the world had always seen me as male, never as a female, despite my efforts to fit into the box society had designed for me. I was always walking a fine line in handling each situation, trying not to anger people because they had made the mistake; many people became first embarrassed, then hostile, so this was not an easy endeavor. As many times as possible, I would try and laugh it off to avoid the awkwardness for everyone involved.

ELEVEN

During the late 1970's and early 1980's gay life was underground, especially in small towns. Finding community was nearly impossible without knowing someone who might sponsor you. Since during that time no one was publicly out, it was a trial and error process; however, a college campus was one of the best options to meet someone in those closeted years.

Eventually that did happen; I became friends with a lesbian couple who were starting new careers and were fortunately twice my age. There was a plethora of gay history in their lives with my mind becoming the proverbial sponge always seeking more information, asking additional questions. Mary, the eldest of the pair, had lived through the Second World War and came of age in the 1950's. She spoke of the isolation and the endless discrimination combined with the fear of employment loss that lasted a lifetime.

With gay society underground, there were few ways to meet people: perhaps a house party where someone could sponsor you, perhaps in a gay bar in a seedy, crime ridden part of a major city, perhaps at a sporting event in a large city. Even within the gay community there were rules. At the time almost everyone was closeted and needed to remain so. While in mixed company with someone heterosexual, you were never to mention two names of the same gender in the same sentence since this would portray a couple in a homosexual relationship. Work life was to be kept at work, never mixing the two worlds of work and play. How could you explain your life to people who thought of you as deviant? Better to keep things professional, profess to have a roommate because women were always poor and needed help with the ever rising cost of living. You were to maintain a simple lifestyle because you would never have the wealth or security that your fellow women colleagues would obtain through heterosexual privilege.

Looking back on it in the present day, this heterosexual privilege will begin with marriage rights and will continue for a lifetime to include social security benefits, retirement benefits, health insurance coverage and inheritance rights to name only a few. By life's end, the disparity will be in the millions of dollars with those in gay society doomed to a life of a second class citizenship. There will be a lifetime of anxiety to stay employed in a homophobic world. Much of the country had anti-sodomy laws still on the books which meant that just being gay was illegal. Tossed into that mix of hatred was your family of origin who could be as homophobic as society at large. Parents who did not want a gay child were quick to punish their children in every possible way: physical, emotional and mental abuse perhaps combined with the order to leave the family home. The attitude prevailed that we had chosen to live this life of deviance, thus we deserved our second class citizenship. For years, my mother had known I was different, and the older I got the more heated our discussions became. Once I became an adult she let it be known that I needed to leave the area to spare her the humiliation. Of course, I had always had that as my goal; however, my poor health had prevented me from being able to support myself even at a minimum wage job until two years after my kidney surgery.

By 1980, Ronald Reagan was elected president and the country began to change in every way. President Carter had given us energy conservation, government services for the poor, and provided some increased economic prosperity. Once President Reagan came into power, all of that reversed into government budget cuts with increased military spending. His philosophy was that government was far too cumbersome and therefore needed to be downsized. The poverty that began during that time is still with us today. Overnight, the country became conservative and believed that one only needed to pull oneself up by their bootstraps to succeed and fulfill the

American dream. The size of houses began to increase during this decade with the McMansions being built, destroying farmland through a devouring urban sprawl that knew no end. Materialism and consumerism were the new mantras for many of the baby boomers attempting to supersize their parents' accomplishments–bigger houses, better paying jobs and all the toys and contraptions that could be purchased to make life easier!

It was during this time that I began to get involved with the underground gay community while I finished up the last of my classes at my regional campus. Mary had parted from her lover and to survive economically had taken in housemates. I moved in and was grateful for the chance to live life more freely. I began to wear men's clothes complete with neck ties and would frequent the gay clubs that were flourishing in the major cities, hours away. This was just before the plague hit, the clubs full of handsome young men dancing to the disco tunes of Gloria Gaynor, Sylvester, Donna Summer and ABBA. Always present were the showgirls: the female impersonators performing a tune by Judy Garland, Marilyn Monroe, Patsy Cline or any number of gay celebrated icons of the time. The clubs were always in the seedy inner city neighborhoods with drugs and prostitutes easily available. I was approached one night by a hooker, understandable since I looked young and male, but of course declined her offer. Being at those clubs during that time was freeing and affirming for me and I'm unable to hear the music of that era without drifting back in my mind's eye to that last chapter of history that was filled with liberation and no death.

I had moved out of my mother's house but was still stuck living in my hometown until I could move farther away. My underground gay community at the time was a group of friends who were slightly younger than me and from abusive childhood homes. We were all together trying to begin the new decade of the 1980's with hope and determination. We worked hard at minimum wage jobs, drank far too much alcohol and tried to determine who we were as individuals. More importantly, we navigated a hostile homophobic world knowing we only had each other to depend on. There were the beginning lessons of feeling isolated: a young boy talking with Mary and me about his recent breakup with a lover; sobbing as he recalled how difficult it was to meet anyone because of the necessary isolation of a small town. A young girl who was a senior in high school and experienced horrible headaches due to her difficulty accepting her sexual orientation along with the fear of her parent's wrath. When her medical family doctor was called in to probe her as to what was new in her life, she of course never stated what was really happening in her young life and instead blamed the situation on an overload of difficult classes at school. This was the only way to survive during the early eighties.

It was during this time period that Mary, at age fifty, lost her career job, the result of living at a time and place where gay people were nothing but second-class citizens with no rights or recourse for the endless discrimination. The agency that terminated her chose their verbiage carefully as is always the case. A dismissal notice stated something to the effect that "due to not meeting the requirements of the position…" and she was ordered to pack up her office. The command came from a male who was much younger and no doubt wanted someone that he could hand pick for the directorship. I was privy to the vicious letters sent to her by another supervisor, who was female. She was abusive in her review of Mary telling her she was too fat and too old to continue in any sort of sports position within the agency. I was appalled by the hatred and rage that seeped from those written words. Once again my naiveté was showing, unaware that people could be so evil and disgusting to others who had worked hard under their direction for years. However, it was a learning experience for me to see that discrimination and the lack of any recourse since I would have the same experience even younger in my own life. Mary was unable to secure employment in her field despite a massive territorial search and would attempt to start her own business to survive in the recession of the early 1980's. She would develop breast cancer and die within the next nine years; it was heartbreaking for me but once again, a preview of what was ahead for me in my life.

The whole gang that included Mary, myself and all of the young adults were together as a community for three short years. I still own the photograph of all of the young adult girls, all lesbians, posing arm in arm wearing Lacoste polo shirts complete with the trademark alligator. Preppy fashion was all the rage: plaids paired with polo shirts, and Rene Lacoste, former tennis champion turned designer, provided the couture. We were all so young, so innocent and because of this felt strongly that it was our time to right the wrongs in the world. Some of us would end up in public service, some of us in other parts of the country with advanced medical positions, and some to substance abuse. Life took us in different directions, and sad to say we didn't keep in touch but it was the age before social media where communication was through postal letters, with long distance phone calls charged by the minute.

TWELVE

As the first year of the eighties came to a close, there were fifty-seven young men who had been diagnosed with a yet-unnamed infection in the United States that would eventually become known as Acquired Immunodeficiency Syndrome. That year I would discuss the subject in a sociology class that examined intimate lifestyles beyond the nuclear family. Not much was then known about the disease; I knew that it was attacking gay men, thus, I read everything I saw about it, and very little news coverage was available. My mother weighed in and announced that now gays, with this new disease, would need to remain in the closet and not talk about their lifestyles to anyone. Everyone would weigh in on the subject of AIDS eventually with malice and hate. We were just beginning and didn't know yet what was ahead.

In 1983, I would leave my hometown and finish my last two years of college in a major city hours away from where I was born. None of the locations or names of towns bears any meaning; it could be any small town in any state. There are thousands of such places all over the country with the small town way of life intact. That way of life was horrible for me, never fitting in, always being different, always being ridiculed by others. Everyone knew everyone else with barely a degree of separation; thoughts and opinions were unified and closed rather than diverse and open. I do not want to imply that everything about my hometown was horrible; for many people it was not. However, many people like me who lived in small towns like mine also left for the diversity of the major cities.

The morning that I left was one of the best days of my life; it felt like a new beginning, one that would allow me to live my true life. My main campus offered a work-study job that paid $3.35 an hour and I had secured housing in a basement apartment off campus with a monthly rent of $125. I took out loans for my tuition with a few grants thrown in. For the next two years I would live on a monthly income of $400 a month. My car was a 1970 Buick Electra 225 that ran most of the time, and when it did not, I would take the bus. The rich students on campus would need beer money and would sell me seventy-five dollars worth of food coupons to be used at the student union cafeteria for only thirty dollars. The most important resource I had on my college campus was the student health center which allowed me to see a doctor's assistant and receive prescriptions at minimal cost provided I was enrolled in the college health insurance plan. From the age of eighteen on I had been responsible for all of my own medical bills. My health once again was burdened with endless ear infections, strep throat, and the common cold along with the flu. Despite that, the ability to walk down any given street with no one knowing me was the best feeling in the world. Yes, I was alone, lived alone, went to campus alone, never had the experience of dormitory life or pledged for a sorority, but I was at last free of anyone who knew me.

I would carry a full load of classes in addition to working twenty hours per week. The load was almost unbearable with my poor health; if I got sick and missed one or two entire days, I was behind in both financial and academic arenas. If I had any extra time, which was rare, I would sleep or go to the laundromat. My experience on a college campus of twenty-five thousand students in a major city was the best I could have asked for: my personal growth soared. I tuned into the campus radio station and became familiar with all genres of music and would play baroque while studying on a quiet Sunday morning in a damp, dark basement. My priorities were studying and learning with nothing else tempting me; I was there later than my classmates just out of high school and despite feeling behind in life, I wanted to be in college. I alone was paying for my education with nothing stopping me from finishing as soon as possible with the highest marks possible. I was driven and my obsessive compulsive disorder was in high gear.

My last two years of undergraduate school, although difficult with my own self-induced pressure for above average grades and living in poverty, were great years. One of the first places I sought out on campus was the Student Gay and Lesbian Alliance. Walking into an organization that had both students and professors like me was comforting and empowering; I felt strong and confident knowing that I had support from others. My life had taken on a new and healthy beginning.

Eventually I began to make friends who were gay, I attended John Waters movies, and when I felt settled and caught up with my studies, on occasion I would don my black leather jacket, black leather combat boots and head downtown to a punk bar. Music was always a love of mine, and the decade of the 1980's saw a plethora of creative talent. Studio 54 was in operation in New York City as well as C.B.G.B.'s. Debbie Harry, The Ramones, The New York Dolls, Joan Jett, The Tubes, The Pretenders, and of course, David Bowie were all part of my five-hundred album record collection. The punk music scene attracted me as it was on the outside of mainstream society. The eighties brought us materialism, greed, consumerism, and I was grateful for artists professing their disdain for popular culture. Black leather was a fetish of mine since childhood, the symbol of rebellion not to accept what society demanded. Wearing full leather made me feel strong, with everyone more attractive in a uniform, myself included. In addition, there was the rebellion of gender norms by many artists on both sides of the gender coin. The New York Dolls and Joan Jett provided us with excellent examples of thinking outside of the gender box. Combined with all of the music, I enjoyed wearing the clothes that matched my gender expression. Because I lived with straight housemates I was not as yet dressing as male in my evening hours, only in what was considered "punk" couture.

College brought many wonderful things into my life including love for the very first time. Her name was Helen; she was Greek and German, beautiful, very intelligent and radical. While visiting a friend of mine at her apartment, I noticed plastic milk cartons full of books on Communism, Marxism, and Leninism. Coming from my background I had never met anyone so well versed in such matters and each title fascinated me even more. My friend had a new roommate moving in; that was Helen. After a quick introduction, I asked endless questions and the discussions began. Helen was a Greek Philosophy major, another subject I knew very little of but wanted to learn more. There were so many things that Helen brought into my life that broadened my horizons. We frequented co-op health food stores, supported the second-hand economy, bought women's music in addition to attending women's music festivals and lived on delicious vegetarian and Greek cuisine. Feminism came into my life in a big way; something that I should have been aware of throughout my life but of course, never had the knowledge or exposure. "Take Back the Night!" marches were organized through campus and I participated. Women would march in the street together in solidarity; it was far too dangerous for them to do so alone given the threat of rape and violence against females.

Also during this time I noticed an increase in my unwanted male privilege; the world at large continued to see me as male, treat me as a male. For example, one evening while visiting Helen, we were on crisis intervention duty with an emotionally unstable younger housemate. For safety's sake we called an ambulance as the situation deteriorated and required medical attention. The male medics arrived and immediately questioned me about the situation since I was the only supposed male in the house. Helen was livid as she watched the conversation unfold, and she jumped in and corrected the conversation since it was her house and her housemate and I was only a guest. After this incident I was much more observant in how the world related to me.

America's first women's music festivals began in the early 1970's. Of course, I was unaware that any such events existed until I was involved in the lesbian community. However, in 1984 I had the honor of attending my first Michigan Womyn's Music Festival, located near Hart, Michigan, situated on 650 acres of pristine, undeveloped land. Helen and I attended together and camped with a group of fellow lesbians. At times the festival was overwhelming for me, especially the primitive tent camping. Even though I was only 27 years old, my entire body would ache from sleeping on the ground. No men were permitted on the property, except to empty the portable plastic outhouses. Women operated the day to day activities and built the festival from the ground up each year. A small city would be transformed over the summer, the intensive labor completed by a volunteer crew of only women. Towered speakers and circus tents along with endless stages were all choreographed to produce an entire landscape suited to art and music.

In addition to all of the art, there were workshops every hour throughout the day that discussed pertinent topics, ranging from domestic violence to becoming a mother through artificial insemination. In addition, there was an open air market where women could sell their various wares: art, beautiful clothing, jewelry, all complemented by the surrounding forest greenery. Support groups of every kind were available as were medical facilities. Vegetarian meals were served twice a day with all in attendance completing a volunteer work shift of at least four hours. My favorite part of the event was the constant sound of drumming that never stopped; I would wake up to the melody of distant drumming and fall asleep once again to the soothing beat. Tent and recreational vehicle camping were the only lodging available, combined with cold showers and optional clothing. Every breath we took on that land was full of magic, empowerment and pride. Departing that sacred space and re-entering the outside world was difficult, usually triggering a week-long depression for me.

I was still struggling with deep depressions, at times staying in bed for an entire weekend after working all week. My lifelong battle with depression was still with me, despite the fact that I was finally living my dream. In fact, it was Helen who alerted me to the fact that I was an overachiever, a perfectionist, a workaholic unable to relax or play. It was a correct portrayal of me, yet one that I had never stopped to think about; I had to get through college, obtain a professional job and become a member of society at large, and nothing was more important to me. There were only my friends and the knowledge that I could obtain by working hard; I alone had to achieve that goal. Therefore, I never saw myself as anything other than responsible. However, it was during this time that society at large began to start the conversation on adult children of alcoholics. We began to discuss the effects on children who grow up in households that had an alcoholic family member with books being published by various psychologists and social workers employed in the field. Even though I had continued my therapy throughout college, I started to read books on the subject. Occasionally there would be exercises included in the books that would require forced self-awareness and I would include Helen in on the discussion which helped our relationship.

THIRTEEN

By 1984 there were 7,699 cases of AIDS in the States with 3,665 deaths. The gay community had been active since the beginning in fighting the plague with the rest of the world ignoring the problem. In fact, it had only been two years earlier in 1982 when a reporter asked the White House press secretary Larry Speakes if President Reagan had any reaction to the announcement from the Centers for Disease Control in Atlanta that AIDS had become an epidemic with over 600 cases. Mr. Speakes responded with the question, "What's AIDS?" This question was followed by laughter in the audience of reporters and he then answered, "I don't know anything about it...I checked thoroughly with Dr. Ruge this morning and he's had no (more laughter) patients suffering from AIDS or whatever it is." This was a telling summary of how our government was dealing with the AIDS epidemic.

In my college town there was a drive-thru business, very common with students constantly purchasing liquor. Frequenting such establishments on a regular basis I would get to know the staff working there. A young boy worked at "my" drive-thru who was gay and handsome, with blonde hair and blue eyes. One day, while driving through to purchase a soda, he waited on me; despite his ever present smile, I noticed his skin from his throat down into his open collared shirt had an angry red rash, spotted red and purple. Within a few weeks he was no longer employed and I lost touch with him. Four years later when I was involved directly in the AIDS epidemic, my thoughts would turn to that young twenty-year old and I would wonder if he were still alive. Did he have the beginnings of AIDS-related Kaposis Sarcoma, known as one of the AIDS-defining illnesses of the 1980's? How many other young men just beginning their careers who had graduated with me in 1985 were undergoing the same symptoms? All it took was a wrong sexual partner at the wrong place at the wrong time; after all, in the beginning no one knew how HIV was transmitted. The plague was only beginning to enter into my life; little did I know what was ahead of me.

Our refuge from the world centered on the gay bars: a place to escape the hatred and homophobia from society, your coworkers and perhaps even your own family. Discussions along with safe sex talks were being offered at the bars, with concern and fear expressed in how quickly the virus was spreading within the gay population. Emphasis was put on how to have safe sex with creativity as well as eroticism. Little information was coming from the medical community and there was fear combined with blaming the victim rather than offering support. San Francisco along with other cities heavily populated with gays was seeing an increase in violent physical attacks, labeled "gay bashing." In fact, the subject was now being discussed on some of the mainstream national news shows shown on local television. There was an extreme hostile backlash with some religious groups stating that AIDS was God's curse on homosexuals. To make the situation worse, on June 30, 1986, in the case of Bowers vs. Hardwick, the Supreme Court upheld a Georgia law classifying homosexual sex as illegal sodomy because there was no constitutionally protected right to engage in homosexual sex. Open season was declared with the help of this case, and any rights we had hoped to obtain would be gone as we were literally fighting for our lives. Any progress that we had made in gay rights now vanished; the door to gay rights was now locked and bolted for decades to come.

That same year, I would begin teaching in a suburban public junior high school where the hatred excelled in what was a supposed learning environment. While eating lunch in the teacher's lounge, the football coach made the statement, "This AIDS thing is great because it's really going to reduce the number of incidents of homosexuality." Other faculty joined in with the art teacher complaining, "Our son is a doctor and he has to treat those AIDS victims, why should he be put in danger, it's right in the Bible that what they're doing is wrong!" One of my colleagues asked me if I had heard the latest on San Francisco: "Why, it's full of fruits and nuts and even the weather is queer!" My secretary, angry with a male student while I was in the main office, turned to me and said, "He doesn't respect women, his father is a fruit!" That was one of the days that I woke up and smelled the hate instead of the proverbial coffee.

Everyone was closeted during this time in history. No matter what the employment, keeping a low profile with the added double life was necessary for survival. While on the job, we would pretend to be heterosexual like the rest of the world. Once we were free from work, we could be ourselves and seek out the company of those like we were. The most difficult part was of course not responding to the horrible comments so frequently spouted. However, this was necessary in order to survive and keep a job.

Harvey Fierstein's Tony Award-winning play *Torch Song Trilogy* was playing during this time and I attended with Helen and a group of gay friends; I always supported gay culture at any opportunity. The performance was excellent in every way but what I remembered most was Fierstein onstage in a ranting dialogue with his mother. He went into great detail to explain how many talents he possessed: both feminine and masculine. This struck a chord with me; I wanted that same ability to be well versed in as many masculine and feminine traits as I could muster. The world saw us as deviant and deserving of our second class citizenship. The world saw us deserving AIDS because of the way we lived; so many times it was beyond difficult not to internalize that constant homophobia with a dose of self-hatred. In becoming the best person I could be, I would try and stave off those destructive feelings.

Life has no guarantees and after two years, my life changed yet again. Helen and I decided to go our separate ways and I decided a geographic cure was needed. My depressions were interfering with my relationships and it appeared that although we had shared a life, a home, and a dream, we faced irreconcilable differences. Packing up the minimal possessions that I owned, I moved to the largest city in my state. Yes, the hatred and discrimination were still there, but there were more people like me, a larger community, and hopefully a better life. The late author John Preston, who died of complications relating to AIDS in 1994, once said, "Having a hometown wasn't the point. Being gay was our geographic location." What appealed to me was to live in the largest city that I could afford, complete with the largest gay population that I could afford.

Gay life in most major cities in 1988 consisted of neighborhoods where we would choose to homestead together as gay folk, usually in the inner city or in a historic area. Many times the neighborhoods were rough: full of crime, derelict homes strewn about, and the beginning of the crack cocaine epidemic increased both crime and prostitution. Despite the challenges, gay men and lesbians were going into these neighborhoods as urban pioneers, utilizing carpentry, landscaping and various other skills to provide a home that was beautiful even if only in an inner city neighborhood, not the prestigious suburbs. Word would travel and soon a friend or acquaintance would purchase a home within the same area. Eventually home prices rose in value, neighborhoods became more desirable with growth and urban development, all combining factors for a desirable, progressive city in which to live. This movement had been active for decades in every major city in the country, although it was my first time to see it in action.

Before moving, I had a much needed vacation with my childhood friend Dale to beautiful Key West: a first for me. We traveled in a threesome, he and I and his lover Jeffrey, like college students; with a diet of peanut butter and bagels, and an economy car complete with a tent that we had no idea how to pitch. Sun and beaches with the ocean were what I needed during that cold winter; it was in Orlando that I saw my first set of candles in paper bags poolside on Christmas Eve. Luminaries were a foreign concept to me, as well as most all traditions associated with the holidays. We camped on floors and cooked to save money before hitting the gay clubs. Another surprise awaited me as we investigated the gay clubs complete with drag queens lip synching various Christmas carols. At that time, for the first time, I was aware that holidays could be fun when with my own tribe; a holiday tradition was started then and there, one that continues today. Holidays supported with my gay friends, traditions established with a true feeling of belonging all within my community. Much to my delight I had finally found something that took the place of my lonely, depressing holidays.

FOURTEEN

Before the internet and social media there were gay bookstores that were always located in the major cities: the life blood of the gay community that included newspapers, books, and a safe meeting place for perhaps a twelve step support group. While I was in any city, the bookstores were one of the first stops I would make, credit card in hand, purchasing as many books as I could carry, all by gay authors. During this time there was a magazine called *On Our Backs* that contained personal ads in the last few pages, to be devoured at the first opportunity. Shortly after moving to my new city, I picked up the magazine and while reading through all of the entries, I found a support club for women who were fond of discussing the politics of sadomasochism. Before the day was over I had stopped at a post office and sent out a request for information and within the next two weeks received a reply. My life would again take another turn in ways that I could have never imagined.

Her name was Jane and she resided in my new city, an established career woman: brilliant, a musician, a writer, and well networked in all of the many different arenas that a major city would have for the gay population. Before social media, a sponsorship was needed before the keys of the city would be released to any new gay person. Dialogue with Jane began with my usual endless questions; eventually, we began to enjoy our time together with her offering me housing until I was able to secure employment. The situation was short lived however, when her ex-spouse threatened a custody case; that was another day that I woke up and smelled the hate, rather that the proverbial coffee, having previously only read about such matters in books and gay newspapers. Lesbians and bisexual women had been losing their children for decades, and now I was in the middle of a custody threat myself and was frightened. Discussions were rampant with lawyers, a gay parents group, and of course my friends. In the end, I made the right decision to secure housing for myself with only my name on the deed.

Jane was one of the most accepting women that I had ever met, stating that she didn't care which gender I chose; one particular gender was not something she required, as she was bisexual. In fact, she paid for a subscription to the late Lou Sullivan's *Female-to-Male* newsletter for me to explore. The movement was in its infancy then, copied from just an average copier in San Francisco and sent through the postal mail in, of course, a discreet envelope with only a post office box for a return address. Each newsletter would have my full attention as soon as it arrived; at last I was discovering a community of people just like me on the continuum of becoming their true selves. Some transmen preferred to surgically remove their breasts in addition to taking testosterone, while others had full surgeries which included what we referred to as "bottom surgery," a complete physical alteration and shedding of the former body, complete with hormone-replacement therapy. Frequent comments were that as females we had never felt at home in our bodies; some members of the population had been born intersex or having both male and female genitals present. Depending on the parents and medical community, a specific gender may have been requested by the parents or assigned by the doctors in charge, creating a nightmare for the individual involved. During the 1950's, my birth decade, there was little dialogue on the subject.

As my research and knowledge grew, I was able to see that although I belonged in this newly acquired tribe, we were a very diverse group of people. We each took a different journey to discover that we were in the wrong bodies, took a different journey to individually correct that wrong body, and took a different journey yet again, to decide when and how to educate the world about our different lives. Collectively we shared our common bond of identifying as transmen; our lives beyond that were unique and diverse. Relationships were diverse as well; transmen identified as bisexual, homosexual, and heterosexual. In fact, in scanning personal ads designed for transmen, one could find sexual options spanning the entire continuum. For example, a transman could request correspondence with another female-to-male transman, a bisexual (either gender), someone homosexual (either gender), someone heterosexual (either gender), or perhaps an individual who is male-to-female transgender! Even today, people will ask the frequent question, "Who would your sexual partners be?" My answer summarizes the reality that at midlife, if a connection is made with another individual that is what is most important, all other variables being of secondary importance. Of course, we embraced our male to female sisters and would frequently hold events that included their participation. They read their own material written for them and the needs that they were struggling with.

In 1988, I began to dress as male during my free time, matching my gender identity with my outward appearance. Many times I would be seen as male even when I attempted to present as female. Walking into the women's restroom was never easy; women would see me and look at the restroom sign on the door as if they had made an error. Perhaps I would hear, "This is the women's room…" always understanding that more than anything, I posed a safety issue. Men in an all women's space are always seen as a threat, and girls are taught to be vigilant from an early age and rightfully so. To avoid conflict, I would often take another woman into the restroom to pose as my sponsor, someone who could vouch that I was in fact female.

No family bathrooms existed in the late 1980's; society was still in the throes of Reaganomics: supply-side economics which reduced tax rates to spur economic growth combined with the deregulation of the economy and reduced government spending. We had not evolved as a society to think about average citizens with children who may need to use a "family" bathroom. That era was not one to think about the average citizen at all. Conservatism was the only mood the country tolerated, with anyone on the outside considered un-American. Despite this pervasive mood, I would attempt to educate women while waiting in line at the women's restroom. For example, I would take the blame for the way that I looked and explain that I had just completed yard work. I might say that I was on my way to the gym to work out, or perhaps getting ready to paint my porch later that day. Once while attending an arts festival, a woman I was talking with in the restroom line asked my sexual orientation. If nothing else, I was proof that all women didn't look the same or act the same: despite what society demanded, there was a range. While driving to Key West, Florida in the winter of 1988 I was especially concerned with the south being even more conservative. To aid in being accepted, I put on my college sweatshirt, raised my deep voice by at least five octaves, and announced upon my arrival that I was on the swim team. My hope was that I would be permitted to look athletic, and therefore, away from society's norms of how a female should present. Swimming has always been a part of my life; I had taken physical education classes and knew about the sport, rare for me since I was never an athlete. Once when at a restaurant with Jane, someone went to management complaining that there was a male in the women's restroom. We watched the situation unfold from a distance with management not knowing how to handle the situation with of course my departure from the restroom making it safe again. Nothing was done and we were able to dine at the restaurant.

Eventually I had to take the plunge and enter the men's restroom. The day arrived in a large department store: Jane gently telling me that I needed to advance to using the men's room while presenting as male. She was correct in her advice, but I was afraid that I wouldn't be able to "pass" and be seen as a hundred percent male. If the percentage fell below one hundred there would be doubt followed by questions. Gray areas of gender presentation were to be avoided if possible because gray areas would allow emotions of anger, disgust, and the possibility of violence depending upon the situation. My heart pounding, I entered that first men's bathroom as a father and son team exited; they never once looked at me. Once that first time was over, it became easier with continued practice.

Of course, men's bathrooms vary depending on the location, gas stations being the most primitive. One occasion found me inside a bathroom with three other men, no doors on any stalls, yet always the urinals. Not knowing this was the situation until I was inside, I maintained a poker face and pretended to have something in my eye, washed my face and hands, then departed. Always on guard against a situation that would expose my true birth gender I was a quick thinker, ready to improvise at a second's notice. Using the men's restroom in public while still presenting as female in my everyday life posed the problem of perhaps seeing a fellow male in the restroom who worked with me, or knew me as female. Society doesn't allow gender to be fluid; one of the two boxes, checked off at birth, is installed to last a lifetime. To be as safe as possible, I would frequent establishments that were gay or at the very least, gay supportive. This also aligned with my personal philosophy of supporting my community every step of the way; I would hire services I needed from the Gay Yellow Pages, a directory available to our community published by our local Stonewall Union.

My years spent with Jane were rich with tremendous growth combined with extensive learning. The late eighties and early nineties continued with the AIDS crisis; in the coastal cities the death toll was much higher, but now the epidemic was everywhere. Up until 1988, I had not had any personal life experience with the disease; however, that changed that very year. Artists and creative gay men were among the first casualties, although every life that was lost was meaningful and a tragedy. My personal experience with AIDS was with gay men in the gay male community, just as a registered nurse or medical doctor would have their beginning experiences within a hospital or medical school. This was my time to become involved, to learn, to assist in any way that I was able; this was the time in history as a young thirty-one-year-old gay individual that I came of age.

As artists and creative gay men began to die at an alarming rate, many who knew they were infected began to create art in all genres that involved the subject of AIDS: a lasting memorial for all of us to take part in and the greatest of all gifts. Randy Shilts, a pioneering gay American author and journalist who worked for both the gay magazine *The Advocate* and *The San Francisco Chronicle* was one of the first artists I began to follow. His book *And The Band Played On: Politics, People, and the AIDS Epidemic* was published in 1987. Reading this changed my life; with his impeccable documentation I was able to learn the true story as to what had happened, how it happened, and who all was involved. Shilts would die in 1994 from complications relating to AIDS. There was so much happening during those early years, and so much was needed: money, fundraising, direct care, education, outreach, medical services…the list was endless. My youth gave me energy, hope and determination; my job provided me with money that allowed me to give limited financial support to others. As individuals, we are unaware of what the new dawn may bring us, what experiences, losses, joys and sorrows are yet to unfold. As a young child I could have never imagined where my life would take me, or that the world would change in so many ways, but in 1988 I would adopt my new city, begin homesteading and live a life that overflowed with richness and emotion, riding the historical wave that would unfold in the history of our nation.

Robert Mapplethorpe was another young artist who touched me personally. He was known for his sometimes controversial large-scale black and white photos, celebrity portraits, male and female nudes, along with still-life images of flowers: all gave him deserved recognition. However, his most controversial work portrays the underground bondage and sadomasochistic BDSM scene from the late 1960's to the early 1970's. He had documented the last of the gay sexual revolution; captured before the plague, it was a snapshot of gay history that would never happen again. The homoeroticism of his work fueled a national debate over the public funding of controversial artwork. In fact, in the city where I viewed this exhibit there were obscenity charges brought against the Arts Center and director due to the contents of the exhibit. An organization named the "Citizens for Community Values" was involved in the accusations that the exhibit was indecent. As time went on, I would become familiar with more and more of these hateful organizations. Yet such controversy would boost the attendance to the exhibit by tenfold. Lines wrapped around the building causing the viewing of the entire exhibit to take much longer than usual. The slow pace allowed me to study every photograph, observe the beauty along with the creativity, then mourn the loss of this great artist who would also die from AIDS and know most of the photographed subjects were more than likely dead as well.

Jane was active in many different organizations; one of them, the "Gay Writer's Guild," hosted a cocktail party honoring the late author Paul Monette. Since I had not yet read his work I spent the evening listening to the conversations of others. Dialogue included the discussion of the number of famous celebrities who were remaining closeted despite losing lovers to AIDS to hang on to their lofty positions in society: positions full of money, fame and fortune. For those of us in the small cities who were taking care of everything that we possibly could, from fundraisers to direct care of the sick, we found such secrecy appalling. The fight against the plague would never be won with such secrets.

FIFTEEN

During my early thirties, I had the opportunity to explore my inner fetishes and expand my sexuality by learning about sadomasochism. Throughout my life I had admired uniforms of all kinds, full black leather in the uniform style, and sex that involved fantasy and play. Once again, I was involved with a tribe on the fringe of society, and mainstream Mr. and Mrs. John Doe would view me as dangerous and deviant. Education is so important in slaying the fear of the unknown; with knowledge providing power I set off on yet another personal journey.

In 1990 I would join the National Leather Association (NLA) which had officially incorporated after the 1987 March on Washington for Lesbian and Gay Rights. An invitation had been extended to me to attend that famous march in Washington D.C. but I had been sick with strep throat and unable to attend. The National Leather Association focused on education along with political activism. Both arenas were much needed in the still conservative Republican-run country. Individuals who practiced sadomasochism consensually and privately were being arrested. The UK Operation Spanner Case had just unfolded in Manchester: a group of gay men were convicted of assault and bodily harm as a result of their involvement in consensual sadomasochism sex. The National Leather Association was involved in raising funds for the Spanner defendants; I was proud to be a member of an organization that provided such assistance.

There were conventions sponsored by The National Leather Association with the first three located in Seattle, Washington; the conferences were a meeting place for a very diverse set of people from all walks of life who explored sexuality from one end of the continuum to the other. My attendance at my very first convention had me feeling as though I was in some sort of dream that had come to reality. People who conducted workshops were Guy Baldwin and Pat Califia–famous activists and authors there in front of me, my excitement barely contained. Most importantly, I learned the differences between kinky sex and abusive sex, practiced negotiations of what I wanted during sex, and developed a jointly agreed upon "safe word" between my play partner and I which would allow me to shut everything down if I were uncomfortable in any way. Attendees came from around the world and from every walk of life; our bond focused on being differently pleasured. The creed was created: "Safe, Sane, and Consensual Adults," to encompass all that we believed in. Also, we were united as one in the fight to allow sexual freedom: to be free of harassment. Before long, Jane and I were giving lectures and demonstrations to anyone who might question what sadomasochism involved; I enjoyed being a part of such an activity to help people get rid of some of the old stereotypes that were so common.

At about that same time I began to become involved with the transgender community. Once again because Jane was an information addict she was able to research events that interested the both of us. In addition, the transgender community had been networking for decades, but I was not a part of it until the early 1990's. First time events are eternally memorable, and my life was becoming filled with them. Conventions were happening all around the country, and in the early nineties I attended for the first time. Male-to-female attendees outnumbered female-to-male attendees by a substantial margin with attendance totaling around two hundred people. Spectrums ran from those self-identifying as crossdressers, to those who had already had all surgeries, and left their previous genders behind to begin a new life. Of course, there were many who fell somewhere along that spectrum and wished to remain where they were most comfortable.

My excitement that weekend was uncontainable with at last attending a convention that would supply me with workshops, resources, education, and the opportunity to network while socializing with others who were like me. Arriving at the hotel, my first encounter was with a group of male-to-female crossdressers engaged in a lively cocktail party. When I introduced myself as one of the transgender attendees who was female-to-male, they did not believe that underneath my suit and tie I maintained a female body! Just as the world had always viewed me as male, my own people were having difficulty imagining me as anything other than male housed in a male body. Determined to cruise for my first female-to-male person that I would see firsthand, I quietly stayed in the background and watched as attendees came into the hotel and began to register. Eventually it happened; I was able to spot someone like me but with facial hair and a flat chest from surgery. He caught me cruising him and started to turn around to look at me again as I bolted down the hall to my hotel room trying to hide my excitement.

The next morning we would meet and he would disclose his journey to a small group of females who were never comfortable in their bodies. Discussions were abundant that weekend with each of us bringing our stories of our own journeys through life. Common themes included the loss of employment through discrimination, the loss of family, depression brought on by the knowledge that our gender was not how we thought of ourselves inside. We came from all across the country seeking refuge from the storms of those who chose to hate and reject us; we sought comfort among our own with those who understood.

The weekend concluded with a formal dance in the hotel's ballroom. As I was escorting Jane down the hall, a male turned to me as we rounded the corner and said in a disgusted tone, "There are a lot of faggots in this hotel this weekend, aren't there?" His disgust reached fever pitch as he watched us head into the ballroom where all the so-called "faggots" were congregating. I ignored his comment and focused on the event that was so wonderful for the both of us.

Another vivid memory from that weekend involved a crossdresser who served as an officer in the military; during brunch the following morning she discussed a conversation she had with one of her men in a combat zone. One of her fellow male soldiers had asked her what she would be doing on this particular day and hour if she were stateside. Of course, she told us that she would have been at a "tea party" with her fellow crossdressers but softened it a bit with her men and described a golf game instead. As I looked to the side of the dining room, I could see all members of the kitchen staff lined up listening: some in disbelief, some with mouths agape, and some with quiet disgust. Republican president George H.W. Bush was in office and the country was involved in Desert Storm: once again, it was another period of conservatism, war, and less than a liberal time in the country.

Leaving the convention that following afternoon, grateful for all of the support and contacts that I had made, my mind was spinning. What I had thought about my entire life had come to fruition; there were others just like me, support, and medical options all begged nagging questions. Where would I go next, when would I transition, was it something to venture into or just think about in this new chapter of my life?

SIXTEEN

As outcasts and deviants, we came of age in our respective communities with the mentoring of our elders. Many of our own families wanted little to do with us; we created our own support systems through various organizations. Because I had always bonded with gay men since the age of nineteen, I wanted to continue that avenue of support in my newly adopted city. Jane was involved in a plethora of organizations and would sponsor me to various events taking place within the city, including gay male clubs.

Gay male clubs have had a long history in our nation, and of course in the early years were underground. My first knowledge of the history was from reading Guy Baldwin's article in issue 150 of *Drummer* magazine from 1991. Baldwin discusses the earliest gay male clubs that began after World War II: gay veterans who wanted to retain the most of their homosocial experiences, which involved being thrown together in the company of other men for significant lengths of time and away from their hometowns all for the first time. War is a horrible event: one that is never forgotten. In addition, the gay vets were aware of the fact that although they had been closeted, they had fought just as hard if not harder than their heterosexual brothers. The values of hard work and discipline were learned in the accomplishment of an honored goal. Working hard and playing hard were all part of the soldier's life during wartime.

After the war ended in 1946, many of the gay vets wanted to retain the most satisfying elements of their military experience in addition to socializing with other gay vets. This sort of camaraderie was only found within the motorcycle culture and so the gay biker clubs were born. These motorcycle clubs involved gay men transferring their loyalties to the same leather uniforms that a motorcyclist would wear with some additional insignia included. Club colors were created to honor the insignia, with members of other clubs exchanging their club colors in a gift of friendship to be hung with pride within their headquarters of a local gay male biker bar. Leather bike caps replaced the military dress uniform hat with the leather uniform replacing the military uniform. The biker bars were a place where they could advertise their sexual preferences in a way that had been impossible to do previously.

Just as during war time soldiers would play the parts of women by dressing in women's clothes for some entertaining stress relief, biker runs followed in the same tradition. Just as the military had the tradition of many rules, so did the biker clubs. Along with that, a sort of ritual formalism was in place to be followed by all members. Elder members were to be addressed as "Sir" and treated with respect as well as dignity. A code of honor involved honesty, integrity, responsibility and looking out for the welfare of others within the club.

As time went on with additional wars to follow, the biker clubs flourished although as always, underground and secretive except to those directly involved. My first experience with biker and what we referred to as "backpatch" clubs came about in the fall of 1988 and has been ongoing throughout my entire life. The "backpatch" was earned and sewn onto the back of the leather vest or denim jacket, displaying the logo and design of the particular club.

During September of 1978 a group of fifteen gay men assembled in an empty warehouse and decided to form a club to foster brotherhood.

Officers were elected: President, Vice President, Sergeant of Arms, Treasurer, Road Captain, Secretary and Pledge Master. The name "Centurions" was given to the club with the first anniversary party or "run" held in October 1979. As the club was forming I was then working in the factories, searching for a direction in my life that was valuable, and would have enjoyed knowing there was support for me despite my outcast status. However, in the days before computers, social media and the like, information was impossible to obtain in the one-horse town where I was living. The major cities had one or two gay bars that might carry that sort of information, but there were no guarantees. In addition, sponsorship was necessary; someone on the inside would be needed to vouch for your character and reason for interest. Communities were all important, the shelter from the storm needed to buffer you from the rest of the world. Historically, this was a time when most were closeted from all who knew them: especially employers and usually parents as well.

With the onset of AIDS in the early eighties everything would change. In 1980, there would be thirty-one deaths from HIV in the United States with the toll continuing to climb from that moment forward. Jerry Falwell among others would announce that AIDS was God's judgment on a society that didn't live by His rules. Remaining closeted was not an option once you became infected with the virus, causing many to die robbed of employment, any sort of benefits, or any support from family members. There was a huge backlash against gay rights; we would lose decades of time in obtaining any rights with millions of lives lost to a horrible death. Polls taken in 1985 showed that fifty-one per cent of Americans favored quarantined confinement of all those stricken with the virus. William Buckley would declare that there should be tattoos on all who had AIDS, to protect the victimization of other homosexuals. Republican president Ronald Reagan in his authorized biography would state that perhaps the Lord brought down this plague because illicit sex is against the Ten Commandments.

Until 1988 I had no direct experience with anyone battling with AIDS, although I had kept up with both gay and straight presses on the progress of the disease. Upon relocating to my adopted city in late summer of 1988, that all changed with my first AIDS funeral in the winter of 1989. With the help of Jane and her diverse array of contacts, we began to support the Centurions at their home bar: Ft. Dix. At this point, AIDS was in every city in the country; the gay community had taken matters into their own hands after viewing the lack of caring displayed by the world. Fundraisers were implemented across the country to raise much needed money for those who needed it. AIDS Task Forces sprang up around the country as well to serve in many capacities: direct care, funding, education, outreach, and the list expanded as time went on. With the assistance of Jane guiding me, I was able to visualize for the first time ever how dire the situation was with so many men infected with the virus.

Jane and I attended our first Centurion run in the fall of 1988; we were welcomed with open arms and support by one hundred and fifty gay men, all individuals bonded by the common thread of brotherhood. During that time in my life I was female by business hours and male at all other times. Most men understandably viewed me as male when they saw me for the first time, and I was constantly cruised in the bar. Always flattered to be seen as male, I never rejected any man's compliments. Should the situation begin to go further, I would express my thanks and gratitude but explain that I was in a female body.

Eventually I was given a male stage name by a Centurion and was invited to be a part of the drag shows that hauled money from the audience in the form of tips to the performers, one dollar at a time, with all tips donated to the benefit charity. Wearing a tuxedo or perhaps full leather while introducing the performers to the audience, I considered the work a true honor that I was delighted to participate in. During this time, I was the only female, (although not yet a member) involved in a gay male leather backpatch club. Four members of the Centurions decided to form a production company that created the shows; rehearsals were grueling with the end results combining camp, comedy and excellent choreography. The plague had brought everyone together to organize, to assist, and to fight for a better life for people with AIDS.

Organizations and clubs of every kind were everywhere in the city: the result of an increasing gay population of young, energetic, as well as urban people who were able to work and settle within the city limits. There were three additional backpatch clubs, a country-western dance troupe that won awards in dance competitions, gay sports clubs, gay choruses, to name just a few of the many gay-endorsed functions within the city that allowed support, friendship and acceptance. My life consisted of a gay world, a world where I belonged, where I was accepted for who I was.

However, I was still battling depression and was still constantly sick with a cold, the flu, an ear infection, even a yeast infection whenever I took antibiotics. Nothing had changed with my health but it was so much more tolerable living in a "gay city." Soon my life became very busy, as one's thirties frequently are, with homesteading, volunteer events with the Centurions, and gay culture of one form or another at every opportunity. There was an abundance of culture that came out of the AIDS crisis: plays, movies, literature, art exhibits and many many performances. As a society we were gifted with so much from so many who are now gone. Because I was constantly out in the community and supporting as many organizations peripherally as I had time for, I had a large circle of friends from every walk of life who I loved and who were my family. My city had become my home where I wanted to stay and put down roots with my gay male brothers and the gay community at large.

Eventually I was asked if I would consider becoming a full member of the Centurions; it was one of the biggest honors to happen in my life. My time with that organization was filled with every emotion, with endless hard work filled with tremendous personal growth. Our membership consisted of twenty-eight men in careers spanning law, medicine, education and law enforcement. Also, we were artists, bartenders, state employees and corporate executives. We were together as a unit fighting a cause so much bigger than ourselves but never once thought about stopping that fight. After all, there was work to be done, and we decided to step up and partake in any way we could.

Before becoming a full member one was required to be a pledge for six months. During this time the pledge was under the guidance and mentoring of the Pledge Master: a full member assigned to the care of all incoming pledges. During the six month pledge period a pledge had a chance to experience the organization up close, while the members of the club had an opportunity to evaluate the pledge. After the six months, a vote would be taken by the membership to decide if the pledge would be eligible for full membership. Because the Centurions were open about what was required in full membership to the club, very few pledges were rejected. For the most part, full membership was the equivalent of a part time job that would cost money rather than provide money. Monetary dues were required in addition to the cost of a dress uniform, the cost of costumes and traveling to support other clubs. Membership was capped at twenty-eight full members to maintain the closeness and familiarity within the organization. Those who were unable to maintain these commitments were permitted to go to alumni status to participate as they were able. At times there were individuals who volunteered time, money, and skills to the Centurions but chose not to become a member, and were given the title of Honorary Centurion. Usually there was an honorary member added to the roster each year.

Once a month, on Centurion bar night, all hands were involved at the designated home bar, the headquarters of the organization where activities were held. There was a small charge of two dollars to enter, with all of that money given to a charity designated by the membership. In addition, beer would need to be carried by pledges and members from the walk-in freezer to put into the coolers behind the bar. Each bar night had a theme so decorations would need to be put up, taken down and then stored all in the same evening. Glasses were to be cleared and washed during the entire night until closing; with smoking permitted, all ashtrays would need to be emptied and cleaned at closing.

After the bar closed, all of the membership would sweep and attend to glasses, ashtrays and whatever else was needed to close down the bar. Bar night shifts would begin at nine in the evening and end at around three the next morning.

When it was time to celebrate the anniversary of the club being together for another year, additional work was needed. A hotel was secured; meals were arranged at the hotel and in the local gay bars that served food, with vans rented for transportation to the local bars in the city, to ensure safety while drinking. Security was posted on the hotel floors to ensure privacy from the general public. All who attended needed to be registered and given identification badges from the club. As always the theme chosen would be woven through the entire weekend: from decorations to table centerpieces to costumes by fellow clubs who hosted cocktail parties. Themes over the years included the 1950's, a travel theme aboard a cruise ship, or perhaps a local diner where the waitresses ruled the roost. Pledges were given duties during the anniversary celebration that might include helping attendees unload their luggage, serving coffee to all hotel guests who might request the beverage, or filling a shift that began at seven or eight in the morning to assist with breakfast duties. Activities included a poker run on motorcycles and games that might involve running in high heels to a designated finish line. Another game might be to guess the amount of candy pieces housed in a jar. Creativity combined with socializing were the extended goals with a strong dose of camaraderie. After all of the games were over and packed up, a drag show would be performed complete with endless laughter, camp, makeup and costumes. For those members who felt that they would melt if seen in a dress, there were other endless tasks to be completed: filming the performance, assisting in stage crew, assisting back stage and other duties as assigned.

Centurion shows were the pride of the membership with hard work required in rehearsals, props, costumes, lighting and music. My career on stage started in a formal tuxedo but as the years went on, I began appearing in female costumes as well. It was fascinating to my fellow brothers as I appeared in feminine costumes arranged by my show director; his vast knowledge of both cosmetology and choreography kept me looking and moving at a higher level than I had ever known in my life.

Productions were three times a year: the anniversary run in September, the bar's anniversary in November and a Christmas show to culminate a huge campaign that began five weeks earlier.

After the anniversary show in November it was on to the holidays and providing money to five children's charities, decided upon by all members. Activities to generate money would be guest bartending at another gay bar, and providing our teddy bear mascot copied onto a paper picture to be colored and then displayed in the bars. Patrons loved to color and return to their youth as calm crossed their face, crayons in hand, with fierce concentration, soon to complete their art for the teacher/bartender to display for all to see. Many of the paper teddy bears bore the name of someone who was no longer with us yet still remembered. Centurion members and especially pledges would don a teddy bear costume to visit various gay sports arenas (the bowling alley, and the dart league) to gather monetary donations for the children.

During that time, there was a children's AIDS unit housed in the local children's hospital. Previously, during the Teddy Bear Campaign, members had attempted to provide stuffed teddy bears for the children who were sick in the AIDS unit; however, because of the lack of sterile conditions within the bar, the idea had to be abandoned, replaced by cash. However, in the early years when toys were still collected, the common practice was to fill a pickup truck full of bags of toys to be delivered directly to the hospital.

During a Teddy Bear campaign after the millennium had arrived, I was attending bar night with my brothers at a guest bar. Frequently other bars would request that we attend donned in our club colors to provide increased visibility to generate additional support. We were in a section of the city that was rife with poverty, housing people who were working two jobs just to survive. A woman walked in and with glee stated, "I didn't know the Centurions were going to be here! You all gave my baby a teddy bear sixteen years ago when she was in the hospital and not expected to live through the night. You know, she still has that teddy bear and she's doing fine now. You ought to see how big she is! I'm so glad you're here tonight; I always give money to the Centurions whenever I see you out in the bars." With tears streaming down my cheeks, I was able to share that moment of happiness with her and was even able to say a few choked up words of how much her story meant to me.

Christmas was a time full of emotion: the happiness of providing help for the children combined with the tears at the end of the drag show. All members of the Centurions along with cast members would be onstage after a profitable night of fundraising. Each year would bring in more money than the last. Some years would bring in as much as ten thousand dollars, one dollar at a time. As we all stood on the stage together, we would sing Bing Crosby's "White Christmas" with the audience. Tears would flow, for the pride in helping others, the raw pain for those who we had lost, along with the reality that there were brothers who were sick and would not make it until the next Christmas. Attendance at the Christmas performances always broke the fire code that restricted how many people could be in the building safely. It was standing room only, beyond crowded with both straight and gay people in attendance. Somehow during the Christmas season all hatred was set aside with the focus only on helping the children.

Other clubs in the city would volunteer to perform as well, with people donating their art to be auctioned off in between performances. Each year the show would grow to be longer than the year before but with more money raised.

Before we closed out the 1980's, in 1989 the film *Longtime Companion* was shown in one of the more liberal theaters. The title reflected the verbiage used by *The New York Times* to describe the surviving same-sex partner of someone who had died of AIDS during the 1980's. This film was the first wide-release theatrical film to deal with the subject of AIDS. The film begins with a group of several gay men on Fire Island, on July 3, 1981. *The New York Times* had just published the article warning of the rise of a new gay cancer. We watch as the news spreads throughout the group of gay men as they phone one another to discuss the article. As the film progresses, we watch as these same young successful men begin to die, with footage that is raw, realistic, packed with heart wrenching emotion. The film showed the audience the undeniable horror of all that was involved with losing those we love to AIDS: fear, discrimination and constant needed care as the disease progressed. Above all there was the intense sadness that never stopped; I was in tears for the majority of the film as was most of the audience. For the late eighties, this film was groundbreaking and timely; it brought those emotions to the forefront of our lives: we all knew there was much work needed ahead.

SEVENTEEN

As the nineties began, there was hope that had not been present for at least a decade. After the conservative eighties, complete with the religious right in full voice spewing hatred along with bigotry at every turn, a democratic president was at last elected. President Clinton unlike his predecessors was aware of the AIDS epidemic; however, by this time more and more organizations had gotten involved in the fight against AIDS.

A very successful organization was the AIDS Coalition to Unleash Power, better known as "ACT UP," which had been formed in 1987 in New York City. This diverse organization was historic in their ability to get drugs into bodies, change legislation and reduce pharmaceutical prices for much needed drugs. Decades later, I would read the ACT UP archives online and realize how much change came about due to the focused rage of this group of dedicated warriors. Many of those involved in ACT UP were at one time closeted but after contracting AIDS were forced out with nothing to lose. Many had lost their powerful careers; this caused them to focus on fighting for their lives. They were outraged at the way both local and national governments were ignoring the growing number of deaths.

Unfortunately, the AIDS epidemic was extremely complex; the gay community was very protective of the liberal sexual lifestyle that had prevailed since the Stonewall riots. When officials wanted to close the bath houses, there was anger with the fear that it would be the beginning of the loss of rights that might end in quarantine for everyone who had AIDS. The community began to become divided, providing the two camps of those who were positive and those who were negative. There were debates within ACT UP in New York City because there was so much work needed in so many areas to facilitate change. Members were involved three to four nights per week to participate in various committees, with burnout rampant from all that was involved.

My mother sent me an obituary of a childhood friend that I had grown up with who attended my Kingdom Hall. His name was David; he was barely nineteen, and had moved to San Francisco a year earlier and was working as a florist. There was no mention of the cause of death; families were eliminating this information because of the stigma involved. When I questioned my mother why the summary excluded the cause of death she said it was to protect the family. By this time I had been to at least ten funerals that were run by the families of my brothers.

The services were conducted as the families wanted, with their religious agenda enforced, without any consideration for their sons' lives. Informing my mother that I would be in charge of writing my own obituary, I sat down that night and completed a list of my life's gay accomplishments up until my third decade and finished the night making a recording of all the music I wanted used in my nondenominational service.

Every loss was different with some of the men going home to families: some voluntarily, others not voluntarily but far too sick to protest. At times, as Centurions, we were barred from the funeral by the family; after all, according to some of the families we were the ones who infected their son with AIDS. Men who had been lovers with someone who had died of AIDS would find the home they shared taken away by the family members of the deceased. We had no marriage rights with families able to use this to their advantage. Also, death is an individual experience with each person to decide how to face the inevitable. Some preferred to be alone, others wanted to leave surrounded by friends; however, up until the end I saw nothing but strength with dignity. No complaining, no bitterness and usually very little discussion of treatments attempted or failed, only the will to carry on.

Although there were many, many fundraisers going on at any given time, hosted by various hard working organizations, I was involved mostly with the Centurions. There is only so much time, money and energy available in any given day; also, I loved my brothers and preferred their company. We were hardly the "Gay-A" or even the "Gay and Professional" segments of the population that existed in every city. Because we wore black leather, produced drag shows and rode motorcycles, we were on the fringe of gay community. In addition, there may have been some fear of the unknown involved since we looked rather intimidating when we were all in leather; some thought we were a club that had endless sex parties laced with alcohol. Yes, there was sex and alcohol, especially when other clubs participated in our celebratory anniversary run. However, it was minimal, with the main focus on the hard work that was required to produce the celebration, not to mention the money that was raised for charity. While judging a leather contest in another city, a lesbian asked me how the Centurions allowed me to become a full member; still assuming it was a closed organization for men only. For a time, I carried a bit of notoriety: an only female in an all male club. I was always grateful for a teachable moment; I would matter-of-factly state that membership was in fact open to anyone who wished to join.

The nineties was a decade filled with political protests; I had the honor of participating in a few of these life-changing events. In 1992, I traveled to Washington D.C. to view the AIDS Quilt, a blanket of art that filled the Mall. Each panel represented a person lost forever, which was emotionally overwhelming to view from atop the Washington Monument. Going to the top floor of the monument and jumping a barricade that read "Press Only," I was able to see the magnitude of horror in lives lost. Later as I walked around the quilt and studied the art, pictures, names and ages on each quilt panel, I could not stop crying. To read the numbers on a page was abstract, logical, even data based; to view pictures, art, clothing, to study the lives of those so young, was literal and told the human story. People were crying with some fondly touching a souvenir or piece of memorabilia to connect one last time. The AIDS Quilt traveled during the nineties, and I would see smaller versions at later times. While we viewed the panels, volunteers would read the names of those lost: the only sound.

Films on the subject of AIDS continued with the Hollywood production of *Philadelphia* in 1993. It was one of the first mainstream films that acknowledged both AIDS and homophobia; Tom Hanks played the main character and would win an Academy Award for his excellent performance. In addition, Bruce Springsteen would win an Academy Award for his song "Streets of Philadelphia." As a community we were grateful for the acknowledgment from the academy. However, viewing the film in the theater was a different experience for me; when Tom Hanks announces that he has AIDS, there was snickering and laughter in the audience. Despite my disgust and rage, I ignored it and tried to focus on the fact that it was groundbreaking for a movie with this subject matter in 1993 to be shown in a neighborhood theater. Once again, here was a film that realistically focused on AIDS with the discrimination in employment that followed. The events in the film were based on a true story of events in the lives of two attorneys. Employers could legally terminate at will when discovering an employee was HIV-positive. We were at last making films on this subject for viewing by the general population hopefully educating them about our lives. Viewing the film was full of emotion for me; I was full of rage one minute and in tears the next minute.

Throughout the beginning to mid 1990's I was catching up once again: this time on my gay history. Tony Kushner's *Angels in America* and *Perestroika* were released in 1993, the recipient of many well deserved rewards. Kushner gave us a snapshot of the country at the time: AIDS during the Reagan years complete with all of the political and social issues of the day. Sitting through both performances was once again difficult for me because of my personal connection with the plague along with the prejudice and hatred that we were all feeling during that time. Yet another example of stunning art that was created to showcase the AIDS epidemic and document the era that is now past history.

The summer of 1994, while at the Michigan Womyn's Music Festival, I met up with the late author and activist Leslie Feinberg. She was there with Minnie Bruce Pratt to honor "Camp Trans." The camp was located across the road from the Women's Music Festival to protest the "women born only" rule that guided gender policies for who was permitted to enter the festival. The property that housed the festival had been sanctioned as women's space only. Due to the fact that male-to-female attendees had not been "born" women, they were not permitted to attend the festival. Feinberg, Pratt and all attendees of Camp Trans marched through the festival in protest of the ruling. Reactions were mixed ranging from cheers, disbelief and shock filled with anger. Feinberg had to stop numerous times along the march to autograph copies of her book *Stone Butch Blues*. My book is autographed as well and preserved in my home archives. Leslie Feinberg was a hero of mine; I had read *Stone Butch Blues* and was grateful for an elder who had lived through the era before me who had documented the history. I too identified initially as a butch lesbian, close to my drag queen sisters. Much of the discrimination that Feinberg wrote of was still alive and well during the 1980's and 1990's: AIDS had brought an entire new era of hatred and discrimination.

Also in 1994, New York City would host the twenty-fifth anniversary of the Stonewall Inn riots. Marching with over a million people in the streets, we were demanding our rights that were denied us. These rights included repealing "Don't Ask Don't Tell," an increase in funding for AIDS education, ending discrimination in foster care, custody and adoption, and a civil rights bill to name only a few. We marched past the United Nations Building and into Central Park. The New York City Gay Men's Chorus sang as they marched in perfect step. As they flowed past me, I felt the pride that we all carried in our hearts. We would gather in Central Park for the rally that challenged us to be a part of the change that was needed. I left New York City feeling energized, ready to take on the needed work that was ahead of us.

Tom was in between jobs when I met him, a fine two-step dancer who would always be with his club at our home just before I was to start my bar night with the Centurions. We struck up a strong friendship and eventually we were in a drag show together camping it up with a number by K.D. Lang when she was singing country tunes. His positive attitude and sense of humor molded him into a person with much to offer. He would often talk about nature and the birds nesting near his front porch who would return each year: he took comfort in that ritual with the change of seasons. Eventually, Tom grew sicker and sicker and was in the hospital. When he contacted a mutual friend of ours and asked that I visit him in the hospital I went the next day. I walked into his room with tubes and machines everywhere, various beeps attached to screens, a portable toilet placed a foot from the bed with the ever present tray for eating that is always in the way of things. Sitting down next to Tom I knew it was near the end of his journey. Kaposi's Sarcoma covered all of his face and his body weight, as a result of the wasting, was dangerously low. He was also suffering from pneumocystis carinii pneumonia. Leaning over, I hugged and kissed him and complimented him on the selection of beautiful flowers that graced his night table. "I haven't looked in a mirror in quite a while, I want to apologize, I know I look bad," he said. Assuring him he looked just fine, I steered the conversation over to him; his voice was fading and it was difficult for him to speak. Friends had just dropped off the beautiful bouquet of flowers and he was able to name every one.

Hospital visits are always difficult; I would try to remain strong, save my tears and pain until I was alone, and able to let go. Tom and I would have less than a twenty minute visit together; this was not uncommon with the struggle to breathe and the low energy that accompany the final stages of AIDS. As I said good-bye and exited his room, I could see a nurse heading in, a disgusted look upon her face. She was dramatically pulling on the latex gloves that had by now become standard. Many medical personnel in the beginning refused to treat anyone with AIDS because of the supposed risk involved. Food trays were left in hallways; masks were worn with face shields. Personal feelings about treating people with AIDS would surface, especially as the numbers grew larger. Silently I turned away, by this time the flood of uncontrollable tears had begun; I was unable to stop crying so I began heading to the elevator. As quickly as possible, I ran to my car to jump inside and pound my clenched fists on the steering wheel. Within the next two days, I would receive a call with the news that Tom was dead.

Inquiring about the location of the funeral service I decided to attend. Due to getting lost in finding the church I was late and sat alone throughout the service, dressed in a black suit, white shirt and black tie. The minister delivering the eulogy was ancient as were most of the guests in attendance. Tom had adopted a church and remained closeted about his other life; he was not hospitalized until the end and had kept the AIDS diagnosis from all but his mother and gay friends. As the minister droned on and on with his rubber-stamped eulogy I could not stop crying; not just for Tom but for this life that was cut so short. He had not entered his third decade of life; I would never want him to continue on with this horrible disease that was destroying him inch by inch. Instead, I reflected on how young he was, how devastated his mother had been when she learned that he was sick and how many people all around me were sick and going to die as well.

After the service, I joined a mutual friend of ours to discuss the next service, a gay remembrance back at Tom's house. While we were talking, a fellow congregant approached us and with true social grace, I was introduced. Instead of introducing me with my male name as was usually the case; with all of the stress of the day, I was mistakenly introduced by my female name. I held out my hand in order to shake hands with the woman I had just been introduced to. As she realized that I was a female dressed in male clothes, she shrieked with horror and withdrew her hand to stare at me. Attempting to diffuse this socially awkward situation, I nodded and spoke of how nice it was to meet her and quietly slipped away. Crying all the way back into the city, into the gay district where Tom had lived, I arrived at his former Victorian home.

At last with my tribe, I put away my handkerchief and went inside to a solemn gathering of fifteen gay men. What was to be a celebration and remembrance of Tom's life was heavy drinking, unspoken sorrow and fear. Tim, one of Tom's housemates, described a list that he kept in his bedroom that named all of the men he knew that had died of AIDS. Tom had been number sixteen. Attempts were made by all to remember the good times shared before the plague had hit, the alcohol lubricating laughter along with past memories. Although Tom came from a supportive family, many men did not, and upon their deaths the family took over the homes they shared with their lovers. Many times a gay man would return home from his lover's funeral to find the locks changed on their shared home. Families who would blame lovers for infecting their sons would resort to these tactics in their rage. There were no gay marriages to legalize the partnership of two gay men wishing to share property and a life together. Because so many men were dying childless and under thirty years of age, parents were the next-of-kin by law. These were the days of slogans, put on the backs of T-shirts that read, "Gay=Got AIDS Yet?" and "Kill a Queer for Christ."

Paul was a member of the Centurions, who was involved in my life for barely five years: the blink of an eye before he was gone. We were talking once about our parents and he spoke of a father who refused to allow him to take dance lessons, because he did not want a sissy for a son. His father did get a sissy for a son, an artist so creative that as an adult he began to perform as a drag queen in our bar. Paul enjoyed performing as Cher: so perfect in his art, I would have to remind myself that Cher was not on stage. Paul would have excelled in New York City, his choreography and artistic talents were numerous; one performance had him driving onstage with a motorcycle to complete the theme of the song. Despite his father's alienation, his mother and sister supported him with both of them in attendance during our Centurion shows. Paul's lover Carl supported him as well throughout his decline to his death.

Due to his family's support, we were permitted to attend his calling hours complete with an open coffin. Because there were so many preferred cremations during that time, an open coffin was comforting to me. Growing up with that custom throughout childhood gave me the opportunity to view my brothers one last time despite the difficulty. Before exiting the building I sat beside his mother and sister, choking back tears, reminding them that they were my family and how I would always love them. Carl never left the coffin until the end, always taking care of Paul and the stress of it all was visible in his face. He as well would have the same fate and die within the next five years. Once outside in the parking lot, with a cool summer breeze, I was able to let go, to sob, to cry to grieve for Paul and all of those taken from us.

Nic and Robert were lovers homesteading in a rundown neighborhood of the city. Robert was employed at a printing company while Nic spent his days in a dry cleaning business. Robert was a martial arts enthusiast with the largest collection of photographs as well as artifacts on the subject in the country. Both men were full of life, always displaying a great sense of humor and were both members of another local back-patch club in the city. With time, Robert began showing the ravages of the disease: the wasting of his body, his teeth falling out due to the chemo needed to fight the endless cancers that AIDS allowed to fester. Eventually Robert disappeared from public; such is the decision made by the individual to be honored.

The Centurions would often host bar nights with open boxes to be filled with toothpaste, shampoo, razors and shaving cream: items always needed in the hospice units. Other fundraisers included bake sales, pizza sales, and water sold during the hot summer festivals. All activities added up to money in the charity bank; all volunteer, and all proceeds directly funneled into the charities.

Bob and Dave were lovers and owned the bar next door. Both men were active in the political arena, giving money to charity as well as hosting one of the largest Halloween celebrations in the city. The gay bars kept their gay employees without termination until they made the personal decision that they were too sick to continue to work. Dave would speak to me about losing sixteen employees in the early 1990's to the plague: there was no time to properly mourn, instead we worked to help those still living. We would lose Bob first; I attended calling hours with Jane, the family wanted an open coffin which was surrounded by endless flowers, sent by the many organizations in the city respectful of his contributions. A few short years later, I would attend Dave's calling hours, also an open coffin, with his mother standing beside me remembering her son as a child recalling how he was her easiest baby to parent. Living as a gay person in the 1990's involved what seemed to be endless funerals; with sometimes an entire Saturday morning with nothing on the schedule but one funeral after another. Even now I can drive through the city on any given day, pass a funeral home and remember who had had services there.

Jacob was Jewish, full of sarcasm combined with insecurity, as he attempted to find his way in the world. He was in my life for only two years before we took him to the Jewish cemetery, helped shovel the dirt over his coffin, and said good-bye. When he knew he was at the end of his life, he requested that Jane, myself, and three other men who were his dear friends attend a dinner party. We sat down to dinner within the historic gay section of the city on a warm summer evening; Jacob had a bandana over his head that hid the scars of his latest surgery. The doctors had made a final attempt to insert some sort of medication that of course did not work, so he was sent home to die. Jacob spoke of how he wanted us to be together one last time, and requested that we attend his funeral since it would help his parents in their grief. Holding back the tears was beyond difficult; I was barely able to leave the property before I was racked with sobs. Attending his funeral was just as difficult; I watched elderly Jewish men sobbing as they endured the second holocaust: there was not supposed to be a second holocaust that took their young men away from them with a horrible disease that had no cure.

Michael was one of my Centurion brothers who was President of the club when I first arrived; he had made me feel not only welcome but comfortable in a group of gay men. His funeral was especially difficult with his minister using the opportunity of such a large captive audience to attempt to recruit new members. The rage was difficult to endure as we were always to take the honorable road, remain silent and polite. The fact that his lover was allowed to sit with Michael's family in the family section was considered to be progress, despite the crumb that such a gesture symbolized.

Roger was also my Centurion brother, a museum director from the east coast who would entertain me with stories of New York City. A proud and dignified man, I knew him less than two years before he died. Married at one time to a woman, he had a daughter who came in and made his final arrangements; the last time I saw him he had gone down to barely a hundred pounds, had difficulty walking, and was assisted by his lover.

Jay was barely twenty-two when I met him at one of my Centurion runs, just starting out in a sales job with the Gillette Company. He had moved up from the south and joked that his family had not taken his move up north very well: he had gone past the Mason-Dixie line. The last time I would see Jay alive, we were both at a New Years Eve party, in the gay district of the city. A fellow Centurion was celebrating his retirement with Jay bartending. Jay spoke of his hopes for the upcoming year to be better than the one departing. A few months later he got an opportunistic infection and never recovered; his family took him back to the south and I was unable to attend the funeral or ever see him again.

EIGHTEEN

Despite the losses my life continued onward, with employment, homesteading, and my health all competing for my attention. The 1990's did not allow time to properly grieve during the AIDS epidemic. Those who were dying were not the rich, powerful, heterosexual white people that were needed to put a face on AIDS. Yes, we had Ryan White, Rock Hudson and eventually Magic Johnson; before the famous we just had people whom no one cared enough about to have it matter, except our own community and perhaps at times, some family members.

My lifelong depressions were still present, still interfering in my daily life and wrecking my ability to remain in relationships with lovers. One day in the cool autumn, I was removing tomato plants with only green tomatoes left on the stalks, never to ripen with frost warnings from my backyard garden. Despite the beautiful weather I was unable to stop crying because I felt as though I were killing the tomatoes: causing them to die when there was still life. When I had so much death around me, I was causing more death. Still in therapy, I was working with a therapist who, although excellent, was nearing the end of her required internship and leaving for a job out of state. By this time, because of moving, taking advantage of college counseling centers both in undergraduate and graduate school, along with insurance changes that might not cover a current therapist, I had racked up a number of therapists who had used a number of assorted therapeutic styles. In addition, I had employed three different psychiatrists who had prescribed various medications with none of them helping me. After hiring yet another new therapist, she made the request that I hire a new psychiatrist whom she had professionally teamed with. Much to my delight, this new doctor was on my insurance coverage plan: no small feat.

It was a decision that would not only change my life but save my life as well; I would be diagnosed with bipolar disorder, obsessive-compulsive disorder, and depression. My new psychiatrist was female, young, brilliant, and nonjudgmental, with degrees in both pharmacy and medicine. After I began a cocktail of meds that I was able to tolerate, my life improved tremendously. I was able to go about my daily life without obsessing if I locked the back door or turned off the stove. Also, for the first time ever, I was able to stop a project before it was completed and not obsess about what was not completely finished. The neurons in my head were at last stable, only feeling them misfire when I attempted new medications.

Chemical imbalances within our brains can wreak havoc upon our emotions as can hypothyroidism, an autoimmune disorder that frequently goes undiagnosed in women. All of these conditions were finally remedied for me with medication. My multiple diagnoses made me think of my mother and all of my female relatives who lived at a time in history when there were no women's rights, no medications, no discussion on Oprah that would create awareness of these many disorders. We are all genetic blueprints of our parents with my family's blueprint dark and difficult. How they would have struggled with no resources or support.

My mother and I had a much better relationship after she was in my rear view mirror on the drive out of my home town. We corresponded through postal letters; it was the age before computers when a stamp was less expensive than a long distance call. Visits were short and positive even when I was accompanied by lovers. One of my many therapists stated that it is nearly impossible to return to the nest of the parental home for any more than twenty-four hours, without becoming a child in a parent's eyes. When change is not possible acceptance soothes the pain; my personal life was one that I seldom shared with my family. Our relationship was fairly shallow, and as time went on we drifted apart again. What saved my life was my gay family, my psychiatrist and the constant quest in fighting for what is right.

Joe was another one of my Centurion brothers who was in my life for only five years, yet another blink of the proverbial eye. We were close with a strong bond between us: one that I still cherish. Joe wrote some of the best scripts for the Centurion performances, especially our show Gigantic, a satire on the blockbuster movie *Titanic*. As an outgoing president of the Centurions he wrote a speech that he wanted to share with me. We both knew that his health would not be stable for much longer, despite the endless clinical trial enrollments. His speech described the honor of being able to help others, the family of brotherhood that meant so much to him, with a conclusion for all present to always know that they were loved. We were both in tears before he ended, with the actual Sunday brunch being very emotional.

Sunday brunch was the time for the Centurions to give awards to the club who traveled farthest, the hotel for hosting us, top scores in various games and the introduction of the newly elected officers. Finally, we also announced the highest honor of Centurion of the Year. Voted on through our membership, this was for the brother who went above and beyond the call of duty. This was the conclusion of a weekend full of camaraderie, brotherhood, laughter and a tremendous dose of gay male pride. This was the time when we forgot about the world, we laughed, drank, played and bonded. This was the time that we focused on our community, with every show bringing in heaps of cash for charity. Joe was also voted Centurion of the Year by all the membership with both of us crying when he accepted the award. Within months after his only daughter's wedding, Joe began to decline. A Centurion couple would move into his house to help him; I would accompany him out to obtain groceries along with needed meds with Joe using a handicapped cart since by this time he was too weak to walk. He purchased a Cadillac to help with his constant pain; easier to take the bumps in the road, more room to maneuver his body that had swelled up.

Joe died in the hospital with the standard morphine drip that is issued in the final days. Making it a point to visit, I stopped in one night just as his daughter and ex-wife were leaving. No sooner had I arrived when his phone rang; after he answered I realized his doctor was on the line. Stepping out into the hall to give Joe some privacy, I lowered my head and tried to compose my emotions. Joe spoke loudly to his doctor, asking him if he had met his daughter. He then stated that he was ready for it to be over. There were so many times when I was in hospital rooms with emotions that had to be tucked away until another time, so horribly painful yet it had to happen. My visit that night with Joe was a very short one with me telling him that I loved him and I would stop in the following day. He died that next day; it was December first, World AIDS Day.

There is a deep heartache that never completely goes away; the pain is always there, and it continues to surface as life goes on without those that I loved so much. There will be a song that will come on the radio that will take me back to my Centurion shows within the first few notes of the song. Tears will flow with racking sobs as I remember those days: the best days of my life. Whenever there is a mention to remember those we have lost, I am unable to hold back the tears. Whenever I view a historical documentary reflecting on those years, I am unable to hold back the tears. Soldiers who come back from wars, who lost their comrades beside them, will break down and sob for the remainder of their lives when they speak of the loss.

Pete worked as a bartender at our home bar. Bartenders who worked for gay bar owners were able to keep their jobs; as opposed to the outside discrimination that faced others, many times resulting in loss of employment. Pete had cytomegalovirus and was slowly going blind, yet he still bartended. During staff meetings the staff would tell him where the liquor was placed so that he could continue to work by memory; if there was a tip that he had missed, he would be alerted to the location of the money at the bar counter. His strength and determination to work under horrible circumstances inspired me; never a complaint or bitterness, only the will to keep working in the job that he loved with his gay family. He was a private man; when he died he wanted no service, with his ashes scattered in an unknown location.

David was another long term bartender who was in every drag show that was a fundraiser for an AIDS charity. He was always joking about how bad he looked as a drag queen, especially after he shaved his moustache. He would perform with an old school song, maybe Diana Ross and the Supremes. A song from a simpler time before there was AIDS, back when we were young and innocent. David was soon hospitalized; the Centurions produced a show as a fundraiser to help pay his huge hospital bills. The money poured in from tips that were all donated. David had dropped an enormous amount of weight but was able to attend the show. As the disease progressed his mother stepped in to take care of him; he returned to his small hometown where he died.

Bob was Jim's lover and worked as a truck driver; he was kind, gentle and had a smile that would light up the room. Bob's health was excellent; he always ate well, got his rest and kept his stress level low. He was a teddy bear both in his demeanor and appearance; during Centurion events he and I would always find a corner to sit and talk. Bob was in an accident: trauma forced onto an already compromised immune system can shatter health that has been maintained for years.

The next time I saw Bob he had lost over fifty pounds. It is never good when battling AIDS to have a low body weight as opportunistic infections can rear their ugly heads. As often as I was able, I would clean Bob and Jim's home while Jim worked day shift; often time just talking while Bob turned the television off saying that out of one hundred fifteen channels there was nothing on. The boredom involved with the endless fatigue and fevers can be devastating on mental health. There is no end to the disease; there is only the downward spiral of the body breaking down. I would take Bob to get his medication after washing his dishes. His kind and gentle manner continued despite the constant pain; my brothers displayed an honorable and dignified way to exit: never a complaint or self pity.

Death was looked into the face as they carried on with their lives. Before long, Bob was in the hospital surrounded by his club brothers with his family. Parents and siblings had both arrived; I would watch them come up the hall as I sobbed in an empty room across the hall. His condition worsened, he went into a coma with his doctor stating that there would be no improvement. After spending the day by his bedside with my Centurion brothers, I left to get some dinner. Within the hour Jim phoned to tell me that he had gone; I immediately returned to the hospital to support Jim. The hospital room was almost silent, filled with Centurions and other friends from other various clubs. There were many, many tears, for Bob and all the others who had been lost to this horrible disease. I stood silently at the end of the bed while Jim kissed Bob on his forehead and announced that he would bury him in his baseball uniform: Bob was a member of the Gay Softball League. The funeral was a celebration of his life, complete with endless pictures and members of both Jim's and Bob's families present to support us. Bob's mother made the comment that Bob had so many friends and I assured her that he was loved by all of us.

NINETEEN

Before the plague hit, the nightclubs were always full; there were times when I would know men by face and not necessarily name. As time went by, I might notice that they came out less and less: eventually I would not see them at all. This would happen time and time again, with so many men. At times it was hard to remain abreast of all who had died. Violence against our community continued; I would also bury two talented and young drag queens who were murdered. There was a coffin at the funeral with a fellow performer giving the eulogy; the room packed full of mourners, men sobbing on the coffin. Another day in the 1990's: another decade so full of loss and rage.

Jane and I decided one night to dine out in the city with three other gay male couples. We had all decided to frequent an establishment that was not gay owned but new to the area. As our server came to the table to get our drink orders, we announced what couples would be combining their dinner tabs, since there were eight of us at the table. The server started to take down orders then suddenly stopped in mid air after she realized we were a table of all same sex couples. She abruptly left our table and disappeared. There is always a choice as to what actions can be taken next. Should we leave the establishment after such discriminatory behavior? Should we stay and insist on better treatment? Randy who was seated next to me pulled a twenty out of his wallet. "It spends the same way it does with everyone else!" he exclaimed with anger in his voice. Another server appeared, one who took our orders and served us since we had decided to stay rather than leave. Such treatment was common into the new millennium; in fact, I was once speaking to two of my club brothers at a restaurant when a woman turned around at a neighboring table and announced she was listening to our conversation and did not like it. The group consensus at that time was to depart from her and the establishment.

While walking with Dale one spring afternoon in front of my home a car drove past us with the passenger's window rolled down. A deep voice screamed, "Faggot!" Dale turned to me and said, "Was that for my benefit or yours?" Not seeing the humor in the situation I had worried that the passengers in the car had noticed where I lived. Of course Dale and I together looked like two gay men. Who I was with would usually set the stage for how the world perceived me. If I were accompanied by a bisexual or lesbian who appeared "straight" I was seen as a straight male. On the other hand, if I were with anyone who looked in any way gay I was perceived as gay as well. The situation would vary often times depending upon how much experience the individual had with people outside of the male and female boxes. I could be called "Sir" in the morning and "Miss" in the afternoon all on in the same day.

My home was on the cusp of an inner tier suburb complete with beautiful small businesses. There was a large bookstore within walking distance of my home that I regularly frequented. There was a small section of Gay, Lesbian, Bisexual and Transgender books located there in a quiet corner. However, a good Christian had considered it their Christian duty to cover the selection with Christian books to ensure there was not a gay, lesbian, bisexual and transgender section available! When I mentioned this fact to the staff, they assured me that they had no control in the matter, especially when they were always behind in their duties, and had no time to police the store.

In 1992 President Clinton came into office with huge support and assistance of the gay, lesbian, bisexual and transgender community. We were so very hopeful that with his administration we would at last be obtaining something besides the second-class-citizenship that had been our ongoing lives.

Our enthusiasm was short lived however; after promising to repeal the laws against gays in the military Clinton instead gave us "Don't Ask Don't Tell." This policy was nothing more than a useless crumb to those who were putting their lives into military service. In addition, he created even more damage when in 1996 he signed the Defense of Marriage Act. Once again, these actions would put us decades behind where we needed to be in regards to the rights that we deserved. Clinton may have hailed as a Democrat, but in reality he was Democratic-lite: one step away from Republican ideals.

Also in 1996, protease inhibitors, the second class of antiretrovirals, were finally approved. Within two years, annual deaths from AIDS fell from over 50,000 to 18,000 in the United States. Up to this point, the annual death rate had been increasing by 20% each year. Despite the delayed medical breakthrough, there were many who were unable to respond to treatment, or were already too sick for such treatment, and the deaths continued. There was such loss it was difficult to stay abreast of who was sick, who had died and where the funeral took place. There was always underlying guilt when I would miss a funeral or not see someone in the hospital before they were dead. There just was not enough time during those years; the grief was never ending with no time to mourn.

In 1997, I would turn forty years old complete with a set of knees that only functioned part time. After taking X-Rays my doctor informed me I had knees that were as poor as that of a seventy year old. To combat that situation, I joined a gay swim team. My time was filled with the bright lights of an indoor pool, a sharp contrast to my dark home bar, with the water healing me in every way. The sport helped my depressions as well; never a competitor as my teammates were, I participated for the wellness it brought into my life.

My cocktail of pharmaceuticals would only increase as time went on; somehow I foolishly thought I could conquer my dark genetic blueprint if only I worked harder or obtained more education. Of course, none of those actions would assist me in attempting to fix what I had no control over.

TWENTY

As the 1990's ended and we ushered in the new millennium, the Y2K hysteria arrived in the fall of 1999. I had never given up on the idea that Armageddon would appear in one form or another and thought this might be the arrival of Biblical prophecy. My basement became my bunker: food, kerosene heater, battery operated radio. I was prepared for whatever was going to happen, cherishing what little control I had. There was always the nagging thought in the back of my head that the world, and the condition that it was in, would not last. Therefore, when the hype discussed the outdated computer systems that would be unable take on the new date, I thought it was true. There was also talk of terrorism, and there were terrorists arrested at the Canadian border trying to enter the United States. They intended to bomb the Los Angeles airport, but thanks to an alert border patrol agent, this never happened. Also, there was a discussion that the infrastructure would be shut down. To deal with this, my bathtub was full of water, I purchased rain barrels and collected rainwater. In addition, I collected plastic bags and buckets for toileting needs. Because our banking system depended on computers, I had three hundred dollars in small bills and bottles of top shelf liquor to use as barter. My cocktails of medications were well stocked, along with my canned goods. On New Years Eve, I was dressed in an old army uniform that soldiers wore into battle, complete with combat boots. Much to my relief nothing happened and New Years Day dawned with celebrations all over the globe bringing in the new millennium. I felt as though a thousand pounds had been lifted from my shoulders. However, no one knew of the Armageddon that would arrive a year and nine months later with September 11, 2001.

I would watch the coverage unfold from my basement; our country would change forever after that day. There was a new and heightened sense of danger that we had never felt before, suddenly aware of the globe that had shrunk in size as never before. Frequently fear is laced with paranoia; suddenly there were vast changes in the country involving personal identification. In every area of my life people saw me as male with a female name. In fact, while going through security at an international airport, as I showed my driver's license, the uniformed officer announced, "You're going to have a hard time convincing me you are the female that is listed on this driver's license!" Always ready in a millisecond for the world to challenge me, I explained that I was female-to-male transgender in a polite and nonthreatening manner. He accepted my explanation and allowed me to continue. Traveling alone, I had no one to sponsor me or reinforce my true identity.

Throughout my life there had always been challenges between my appearance and what was on all of my legal documents. For example, if I were to pull out a credit card to pay for an item it was assumed the credit card belonged to my wife. Talking on the phone was worse: I would give my birth name with the caller thinking they had misunderstood. I would be asked to first repeat myself, and then I would be asked to provide the spelling. One young sales rep exclaimed with amazement, "Wow! Your parents must have hated you when they gave you that name!" Other comments were, "Oh my God, is that the name you were christened with?" One of my professors blurted, "That sure is a strange name for a boy!" Other times people would look at my driver's license and then up at me, over and over again.

When I made my decision to transition, I did not take the matter lightly. I had just lost a job and wanted to reenter the job market this time as a male. Of course there would always be that background check that would announce my previous name and gender, so I applied to companies touting their support of my community. Because society at large had advanced in their thinking, there were more and more companies who would hire people like me.

My medical team was behind me: I specifically had chosen a medical doctor who was known in the transgender community and my psychiatrist was in full support of my decision as well. In fact, as was always the case, she was my best advocate, from the beginning of my transition always addressing me with the correct male name and pronoun. Also, after I came in for my appointment donning a full beard and she did not recognize me, I realized in my disbelief that I had taken on a new appearance. How could someone who knew of my every fear, knew me better than anyone else in the world, not recognize my outer appearance?

Due to the fact that I had so many doctors treating my poor health, I sent a form letter to all, stating that I was going to begin my transition. Yes, there were some of my doctors who were involved directly with my community, but not all of them. My transition would include a legal name change and I listed my new male name. Reactions from my doctors ran the continuum. As an example, my ears, nose and throat doctor commented on how this must be an exciting time for me, especially with all the recent changes that I was making in my life. Not expecting that reaction, I asked him how he knew of my community and his response was that he made a habit of keeping up with such things. On the other hand, my dentist and ophthalmologist who were both in their sixties avoided the entire situation. They never once mentioned my transition and never spoke to me again by name. The remainder of my doctors called me by my male name and never spoke of my transition. None of the reactions surprised me; I knew I was outside of anything they had been taught in medical school.

My coming out process did not end with my own doctors but would include every medical professional I would come in contact with. Because I was transgender, I felt that it was my responsibility to inform all medical personnel so there would be no surprises during the many procedures I was required to take part in. For example, before going into surgery, I was required to have my heart monitored with a simple EKG. This was being performed in an office full of staff I had never seen before. The staff performing the procedure was a retired male fire fighter and I would be required to take my shirt and binder off. Before this happened I explained that I was transgender and even though I looked like a male, once I took my clothes off I had a female body. His response was a gruff, "I've never heard of such a thing!" Thus began the many comments that I would hear from various medical personnel. During one doctor's office visit, a young technician entered the room who I had never seen before. After explaining my situation, she burst out, "You know, you people want to get married, well let me tell you, I don't care, get married!" Another time I was in an emergency dental practice with a young female dentist. Once again, I explained my situation with her responding in an arrogant, demeaning voice, "What do I care what you are!" That same comment was repeated to me once again by a young male doctor, complete with the arrogance thrown in for good measure. Then again, when I hired a new ophthalmologist and described my situation, her response was, "Wow! That's so cool, how old were you when you realized that? My sister is gay and she was finally able to legally marry her long time girlfriend." Despite the comments, I now at least had a male name and looked male with my clothes on. Previous to that, when I had a female name, doctors and medical personnel would look at me, look at my female name on the chart and leave the room. They had always thought that they had the wrong patient and I would have to chase them down the hall, once again explaining my situation. As far as I was concerned, things were now easier because I had a male name and looked male. Medical personnel would now at least enter the room which was more than they had done previously.

Reactions from my friends were all positive; they had supported me unconditionally from the beginning and the transition was no different. However, some of my friends who had known me for decades noticed that my baritone voice had become deeper. I came home one night to find my childhood friend Dale on my answering machine exclaiming, "How many hormones are you taking these days! You were on the answering machine and I didn't recognize you. Your voice is so deep I thought you were my mechanic calling about my car!"

High school class reunions had more of my childhood friends announcing their support; some of them announced that they had always known that I was transgender from a young age. Often, they gave me the impression that they knew this day would come and they were glad to see that the day had arrived.

Pronouns and the new name can be difficult for people and this was an area that I was very relaxed about. Changes require time and practice as everyone around you also transitions with you. Many of my friends who had known me for decades took some time to fall into the habit and I understood that. My previous name and gender had been a part of me for forty-five years and I did not feel the need to destroy pictures or my scrapbooks as a part of my journey. When it came to my sister, I specifically announced that she need not partake in my new name and gender until she was ready. This action helped tremendously especially with her children, and within time the situation was fine for everyone.

By 2003 I would go to court to secure a legal name change; however, because I was only on testosterone and had no altering surgery I was not permitted to change my gender marker. Surgery was not for me for a number of reasons. First of all, throughout my entire life I had been poked, prodded, and cut repeatedly due to my poor health. I hated the operating room, hated all of the surgeries. With a binder I was able to conceal my breasts, and so had that option. In addition, at the time of my transition, insurance companies were refusing to pay for any surgery involved in sexual reassignment. Therefore, the burden would be on me to pay out thousands and thousands of dollars that I did not have. This was just one of many discriminatory practices that the medical community and the insurance companies endorsed. So, not having any surgery would affect both my driver's license and my passport. The laws at the time did not allow gender markers to be changed without a certified letter from a surgeon. This situation could be trouble if stopped by law enforcement, especially if that police officer had not had sensitivity training, especially training that would include dealing with members of the Gay, Lesbian, Bisexual and Transgender communities.

While attending a leather event in West Virginia, I was pulled over by local law enforcement for driving left of center. I was driving left of center because it was 2:00 A.M. and I was exhausted. My partner was worried that a simple traffic stop might escalate into a night in jail, depending how local law enforcement would react. As a flashlight was guided into my face I carefully took out my required drivers license and registration. I carefully explained to the local police officer that I had been tired and thus, weaving left of center. He commented that it appeared I had not been drinking because he didn't smell anything. Apologizing for my poor driving in a calm and sincere manner was enough for me to get released with only a warning. Because he did not look at my license that closely, he missed the fact that I had a male name with a female gender marker. Considering myself extremely fortunate in that situation, I drove carefully away. Situations such as these depend on so many different variables; other transgender individuals have had trouble with law enforcement given this same scenario.

Later that same year, I took some gold jewelry that I no longer wanted into a store that would give me cash. Once again, I was required to submit identification; however, the staff person studied my license this time around. He looked up at me and commented, "The Bureau of Motor Vehicles has you listed on your license as female, are you aware of that?" Thinking quickly I quipped, "You're kidding! Well I need to have that changed!" To my relief nothing more was said on the subject.

Many activists have been involved in the progress that we have made as a society; education with outreach is required to complete the process. Hatred and prejudice take many avenues; however, that is frequently stripped away when they see those who are different as just people. Searching for a common bond with others is the beginning of building a bridge to understanding. Small groups or perhaps one-on-one dialogue have proven to be a successful method in reaching others. Each situation is different; at times a protest or a boycott may be more effective.

Within the next few years the laws would finally change to allow the gender marker to read male to go with my name change. This was due to activism from the transgender community meeting with state officials and showing the need for such action. Also, society as a whole had more of the younger generation coming of age who did not have the prejudice that their parents might have had.

When my gender marker and name both matched, life became much easier; however, I was always aware of the fact that I was not the average male but instead a transgender male. There was always an off chance that my true identity might be revealed: perhaps in the summer when my breast binder could be seen, perhaps someone recognizing me from my past life. As time went on, this became less and less of a concern for me; I grew confident in my new life, and the inside at last matched the outside.

Starting testosterone therapy was an exciting time as I observed the changes in my body; I was finally becoming whole, less fragmented. Never one to want needles entering my body, I opted for the gel that could be rubbed on once a day. Due to the cost involved along with the ever-dreaded testosterone-induced-hormone-rage, I took only half of the prescribed dosage. My lab results would have me coming in as lower than normal; however, that was the best dosage for me.

Even then, I was able to produce a bit of a beard in addition to still having a full head of hair. Our genetic blueprint will decide whether we will go bald and both of my grandfathers were bald for as long as I knew them. If that is to be my fate in the future, I knew that was a possibility. In addition, our ethnicity will decide how thick out beards will be and due to my German ancestry, my beard is thin and wispy.

Testosterone made me feel less afraid and therefore more confident. Many of those feelings were perhaps immersed in the knowledge that I passed as male much easier. This factor alone raised my confidence level but then there were feelings of more impatience, such as driving in traffic and dealing with incompetent drivers.

Support groups have always been a part of my life and my transition was no different. I loved meeting with other transgender individuals from all walks of life. Because I had transitioned so much later in my life, the transmen I met were usually a generation younger. They came from supportive families and at times they had parental monetary support for their surgeries. Also, because they were so much younger many of them were on their way to other cities to start graduate school. Some of them were leaving to start over again in another city after their surgeries were completed: a fresh start where no one knew their past history. Post transition is another journey sometimes, with each person deciding their own path.

Around this time in the leather community, membership in the back patch clubs began to decrease. We had lost two thirds of our membership at this point to AIDS; a generation had gone with no one to replace them. Also, by this time we were losing members to cancer and other diseases. During this time, I had the honor of hosting a funeral at my home with the death of one of my Centurion brothers. Larry had died of cancer, a brilliant scholar with a doctorate in British Literature. He had been storing his motorcycles in my garage and his lover David thought it appropriate to have a celebration of his life near his beloved motorcycles. David played Larry's opera music that he loved and turned his boots backwards on his motorcycle: a symbolic gesture representing loss. Food was brought in along with a beautiful picture of him that was placed above his motorcycles. On a beautiful November day people came from all over the state to honor Larry. We spoke of cherished memories sprinkled with laughter and celebrated his life. Also during this same time, the world was changing with the need for community among younger people becoming less of a priority. The country was at war once again; there was a new enemy to fear and everyone was finding their way in the new post-September 11 way of living. During this time, some leaders within the community attempted to resurrect leather contests as a way of bringing leather back into the community One of my Centurion club brothers who had bee spearheading this effort approached me and asked if I wou consider entering a state leather contest.

Leather contests had been around for decades as a trib to honoring those in our community who strived to ambassadors: working and problem solving in brir communities together, building bridges, educating, prov outreach where needed. Also, contests were an avenue to people together; to celebrate the pride of our culture. Pa judges were secured while promoters would advert contestants who wished to compete. For years I had a and enjoyed leather contests; they were an opportunity my finest leathers while socializing with my family mer the community.

The components of a leather contest involved public speaking and a sexual fantasy scene, all to be p before a panel of judges and a live audience. Also, t some surprise questions thrown in to see how well a could think on their feet. Apparel and public spe always been passions of mine; the most challenging for me would be my sexual fantasy scene.

Public speaking in a leather contest would inv worthy of discussion. For example, the rising numb positive men under thirty: a problem in the gay male community. How could this situation be addressed? The challenge is to be identified with a plan to tackle it, all within a five minute period, before an audience along with a panel of judges. In addition, a sexual fantasy scene is required, with no more than five minutes to perform in front of all judges and the audience. Also, apparel appropriate to one's fetish is to be worn during the apparel portion of the program. For example, because I have a fetish for cowboys, I would wear my chaps over my jeans, hat, western shirt and boots: my fantasy of riding out of the Wild West.

Gathering my club brothers, I brainstormed what I might do; I wanted to create something fun and entertaining. Using my favorite music as a reference point and creating a fantasy scene involving my fetish for boots with two men seducing me was soon ready for prime time. My music would be from my childhood: Nancy Sinatra's 1966 hit, "These Boots Are Made for Walkin." As a child, I had loved the song; as an adult I realized it was more about my fetish for boots. Props included a mock boot store with two male clerks who would fawn over me as Nancy Sinatra blared in the background. We had a wonderful time performing just as we had so many times before as Centurions. Not only did I win at the state level, I won at the regional level as well. International competition would have me placing but not winning.

My time as a titleholder was full of hard work combined endless joy. Most memorable was meeting the hundreds volunteers who gave both their time and money to ensure events were able to continue year after year. Tremendous is needed in planning, setting up and tearing down the contests that are held throughout the country. Serving in community was an honor that I cherished, and one that I am involved in today.

TWENTY-ONE

As each of us takes our separate journeys, we each decide where we fit best on the continuum; however, once I became a transgender male I had no desire to ever return to any fragment of female. On the other hand, I feel honored to have lived my life in both genders; after all, we are all a mixture of testosterone and estrogen, masculine and feminine.

Some young people have chosen to abandon gender markers all together, finding them to be too constricting. As the younger generation comes of age, there have been many changes in their definitions of what gender involves.

When changing and modifying our genders we take all of the consequences that these changes bring us. One of the most disgusting events my full transition has brought full force into my life is male privilege. Certainly not the male privilege that men are born into and socialized into from birth; I will never partake in that aspect of privilege nor would I want it. Being born and socialized female, I have always been aware of the stark contrast between the way both genders are treated by society. However, to be at the receiving end of male privilege simply because society perceives you as male can be shocking. The first time I ever encountered it was as a nineteen year old; I called about the work needed on my sister's car which was in the shop being repaired. The ultimate male space of an auto garage had the male mechanic giving me a detailed description of what had been repaired. Of course, I never acknowledged my true gender but noticed at the time how much differently I was treated. My deep voice that I was born with always portrayed me as male on the telephone.

Throughout my entire life I have been on the receiving end of such treatment. Men are treated with more respect and authority in every way possible. In fact, the older the female speaking to me, the more apparent that authority becomes. Women are socialized to react this way; it is one of the saddest components of our society and the way we interact with others. Also, men are much quicker to pat me on the back and share intimate details of their lives with me. After all, they perceive me as one of the boys and thus involved in that inner circle of men only. Conversations that I have overheard in men's bathrooms and gym locker rooms have been the worst. Misogyny is alive and well in every word that is spoken; it is painful to hear and at every opportunity I make that known to them.

A few years ago, I needed a former college instructor of mine to provide me some information on my home that required some research. In that research he discovered my female birth name, easy enough in the age of computers. In fact, that information will always be there and will surface with any background checks that employers utilize before hiring someone. He was horrified when he discovered that I was born female; what was especially difficult for him was that he had no idea about the matter. He very uncomfortably confronted me, prefacing the conversation with his discovery and asking if I wanted to elaborate on the matter. Knowing that this information will always be on the computer, I was not surprised so simply stated the truth. He had no idea and stated as much and then proceeded to ask me if I had "a tool." Conversations that involve questions always get to genitalia in our society when we encounter anyone outside of that male/female box. Obviously this was something he feared or he would not have asked the question.

About two months later, I saw him in public with his wife at a local summer festival. He made it a point to come up to me and introduce me to his wife. My partner was with me and of course we had the appearance of a straight couple. As he introduced me to his wife, my partner was already rolling her eyes in disgust; he was introducing me to his wife to display what he considered the "freak factor." After I was introduced he would tell her that he knew I was really in a female body. Actions such as these go on every hour of every day in our society. Combine that with the violence, increased suicide rates and garden variety discrimination faced by transgender people, to realize a life outside of society's given expectations on gender is extremely difficult.

Although we have made progress in recent years with gay rights including marriage rights, we still have work to do before true equality is achieved. For example, in many states a gay couple after getting legally married can be terminated from their job, simply because they are gay.

I came of age in a world where being born gay defined my life. A world full of discrimination in which I could lose my career as well as my housing simply because I was gay. Marriage rights were not permitted; therefore, I was relegated to a second class citizenship despite paying the same taxes as my heterosexual neighbor. Because of this, I would always be poorer than my heterosexual neighbor. Social Security benefits, inheritance rights, and health insurance benefits were all reserved for those legally married.

Also, the AIDS epidemic brought the hatred and discrimination to an all new permissible height. The world felt as though we deserved it because of our lifestyle. The horrors of the AIDS epidemic are still with all of us who lived through that time. Those whom we have lost we think about every day: what could have happened in their lives and where they would be today. In addition, it was during that time that many states carried sodomy laws stating that being gay was illegal: a crime even.

Because of who I had a relationship with and because I was living outside of what society considered to be the norm, political, legal and moral laws were involved. When society felt that I had broken those laws, society felt that I deserved the punishment. My life was dictated by the laws of the land at the time.

My journey began in the world of gay men with many of them performing as women in the night clubs. Of course, this was before we even had the proper vocabulary. In researching the subject at the library the vocabulary was "transvestite;" eventually we evolved to where the term "crossdresser" was employed. Then, we had famous people who shared their stories of being in the wrong bodies, who were role models. Society was able to observe their struggles, their transitions and their ultimate happiness when the journey was completed. Each of us who are transgender has a story that is unique; we come from all walks of life. Looking back, I feel very fortunate to have had an accepting home within the gay community. Despite the challenges, I feel honored to have been a part of the history that took place. Also, I have no wish to assimilate into mainstream heteronormative society and am very happy remaining within the Gay, Lesbian, Bisexual and Transgender community.

We try to find our place in the world as individuals, comfort ourselves in as many ways as we can, change what we can, and try to survive as best we can. Life is not easy for those who are outside of the mainstream. We have made progress but there is still much work to be done. Young people engage in the world differently than my generation, just as the generation before me engaged in their world differently. We make our contributions big and small in many different ways. Let those contributions continue on and on!

ACKNOWLEDGMENTS

Throughout my life, scores of people have said that I need to write a book about my experiences. There were many people who assisted me along the way in one form or another, each bringing their gifts to the table.

Thank you, Deev, for all of your love, support, and wisdom throughout the years that I have had the honor of knowing you. You were always there with encouragement for me to keep on going.

Thanks to my editors Jan Brittan and Emily Anderson.

Thank you to my childhood friends who were there for me from our neighborhood: Cheryl, Ingrid, Norma, and Deb.

Thank you also to childhood and university friends Dale and Helena. Your inquiring as to when the next chapter would arrive was most encouraging and helped me to keep on track.

Thanks to Bob and my publishing company Biblio Publishing.

Many thanks to my partner for her love and support and for keeping my feet firmly planted on the ground.

To my beloved psychiatrist: thank you for keeping the depression at bay to enable me to have a better life. You were the brightest and the best in your knowledge of medicine and pharmacology.

And finally, to my readers, thank you for reading my story. Throughout the book, I have specifically avoided referring to geographic locations because I believe these experiences could have happened anywhere. This book was written for anyone and everyone who has ever felt different and struggled through life in a small town with no support. My story may be different from yours, but the feelings are the same. I have chosen to tell my story because when I was young, there was a void of stories; I do not want that to be the case today, and I hope my story contributes to a more positive environment for young people who may be questioning their gender or sexuality.

Each generation works to make the world a better place for the next generation. This book is the true story of my life's journey through the time that was my generation's, and I thank you all for reading it.

Lightning Source UK Ltd.
Milton Keynes UK
UKOW05f1029160217

294554UK00001B/121/P